PRINCIPLES OF MANAGEMENT

CLEP* Study Guide

© 2016 Breely Crush Publishing, LLC

*CLEP is a registered trademark of the College Entrance Examination Board which does not endorse this book.

971091515143

Published by Breely Crush Publishing, LLC
10808 River Front Parkway
South Jordan, UT 84095
www.breelycrushpublishing.com

ISBN-10: 1-61433-024-7
ISBN-13: 978-1-61433-024-0

Printed and bound in the United States of America.

*CLEP is a registered trademark of the College Entrance Examination Board which does not endorse this book.

Table of Contents

Theory and Practice of Management

WHAT IS MANAGING ALL ABOUT?

In a broader sense, Management may be defined as working with people and groups of people with the sole intention of achieving organizational goals. From this definition you can see that the word "Management" is not tied down to managing business or industrial organizations. It has been given a broader perspective; Business, Industry, Educational institutions, Political establishments, hospitals and nursing homes, churches and even families – come under its purview. People who manage should have interpersonal skills. Messrs. Paul Hersey and Kenneth Blanchard believe that "...the achievement of organizational objectives through leadership is Management..."

MANAGING – IS IT AN ART OR SCIENCE?

Managing is something which managers practice. They interact with people in an organization with a view to achieve organizational objectives. A Doctor practices medicine and an Accountant practices accountancy. They practice in their chosen fields because they have acquired skills. So, if we view managing as a practice, then it can be considered as an art. A science, however, needs systematic knowledge, crystal clear concepts, rational theories supported by experimentation and analysis. So, if we view management as a body of systematic knowledge, it can be considered as a science.

MANAGEMENT ROLES

Henry Mintzberg classified ten different management roles which can be grouped into three main areas. These are decisional roles, interpersonal roles and informational roles. Decision roles involve strategy and planning. The roles that fit into this category are entrepreneur roles, disturbance handler roles, resource allocator roles and negotiator roles. Interpersonal roles involve interacting with employees and giving direction. Roles which fit into this category include figureheads, leaders and liaisons. Informational roles involve organizing and interpreting information. Roles that fall into this category are monitors, spokespersons and disseminators. Mintzberg also claimed that organizations could be classified as stable, dynamic, complex or simple.

MANAGEMENT THEORIES

Management theories abound. In some way each theory has contributed a mite to the knowledge of management.

Theory	Its import in a nutshell
1. The Empirical or Case Approach	The experience of past situations to guide in the present. Find out why a particular action succeeded or failed by going deeper to analyze the basic reasons.
2. The Inter-personal behavior Approach	It is all about understanding people and their relationships. It mainly deals with human aspects and stresses that if people understood other people perfectly, organizational goals could be achieved without much difficulty.
3. The Group-behavior Approach	In an organization people work not in isolation but in groups. The study of group behavior patterns is to know how groups affect production possibilities positively or negatively. It relates to the study of behavioral composition of groups, which are large, and how this impacts their relationships.
4. The Co-operative Social Systems Approach	As a corollary of the group behavior approach, the Co-operative Social System came into being. It deals with human relationship as a co-operative social system. Propounded by Christian Barnard, the essence of the co-operative social system is the co-operative interaction of thoughts, ideas, wants and desires of two or more people. His theory focuses on both interpersonal and group behavioral approaches and concludes that their interaction leads to a system of co-operation.

5. Socio-technical Systems Approach	Arising out of the co-operative social systems, another approach, mostly credited to E. L. Trist, seeks to emphasize the systems aspect of group behavior. It tries to relate group behavior with technical systems and its relationships. There should be a most harmonious relationship between groups of people (social systems) on the one hand and machines, systems and methods (technical system), on the other. It seeks to establish that personal behavior and group behavior are necessarily influenced by the technical system in which they work.
6. The Decision Theory Approach	This approach emphasizes that a manager's most important function is decision making and therefore decision should be the central focus. A manager goes ahead on the basis of evaluating innumerable alternatives and arriving at a most suitable decision, depending upon the facts and figures, and importantly, the extent to which he was delegated responsibility and authority. Since decision-making is the core, all the other functions of a manager are built around it, so say the decision theorists.
7. The Systems Approach	They view management as a system, which envelops within itself many subsystems, all operating within the total environment. A total unity which is a collection interdependent or interconnected sub-systems working within a total environment. Concepts, ideas, thoughts, principles, theories or techniques (sub-system) in the area of managing (system).
8. The Mathematical or Management Science Approach	The mathematical models form part of this theory. Each situation is fraught in terms of available mathematical models and then analyzes the situation threadbare arriving at a mathematically correct decision.
9. The Contingency or Situational Approach Professor. J. Lorsch of Harvard University was one of the founders of this theory.	It tells us that any manager's performance is directly related to a set of given circumstance or contingency. Some theorists also feel that it takes into account not only situations but also the behavior pattern of an organization. The spelled out drawback is that instead of promoting total organizational loyalty, it encourages departmental loyalty.

10. The Managerial Roles Approach	This is the latest approach propounded by Professor Henry Mintzberg, to observe what managers do and using such observations as a platform for analyzing and concluding on the basis of such analysis, what their roles (i.e., activities) are. This approach has visibility. The Professor studied the roles of many Chief Executives and concluded that they not only perform the classical function of a Manager viz., planning, organizing, coordinating, leading and controlling, but also perform a variety of other functions as well.
11. The Operational Approach	This approach believes in imparting knowledge from every other field of knowledge such as sociology, mathematics, economics, psychology, etc., which fits simply into management.

Henri Fayol was a French theorist who is considered the Father of management theory. He identified six levels of management functions. These levels are forecasting, planning, organization, commanding, coordinating and controlling. He also created the 14 Principles of Management Theory. These principles include labor specialization, holding authority, strict discipline, defined command lines, centralization, consistency, initiative, cohesion and harmony.

Frederick Taylor is credited with the theory of scientific management. The practice of this theory came to be known as Taylorism. Taylor encouraged breaking jobs from complex processes into step-by-step patterns of production. This is essentially the idea of assembly line production. While Taylor designed his theory to increase efficiency, when it was originally suggested it was often used by managers to increase production without increasing their costs.

Edward Deming was a mathematical physicist who became a managerial consultant after WWII. He believed that most production problems originated due to poor management practices, and not employee error. His theory was called TQM or Total Quality Management. There were fourteen points which he included in this theory.

These points were: Have a constant purpose, accept that a higher standard is possible and necessary, eliminate the need for quality checks, consider quality of materials and not just price, institute modern methods of training and supervision, eliminate fear, increase communication, eliminate work standards and quality advertisements directed at employees, foster a sense of pride in employees for creating quality products, educate employees and managers and ensure that managers are dedicated to creating a quality product.

Joseph M Juran was another management theorist who worked at the same time as Deming. Juran's focus was on improvement end project quality and educating managers to do this. His three step process (called Juran's trilogy) included planning quality, controlling quality and improving quality.

THE IMPACT OF EXTERNAL ENVIRONMENT

Every organization has to operate under different external environments. It is within the environment and therefore has to be responsive.

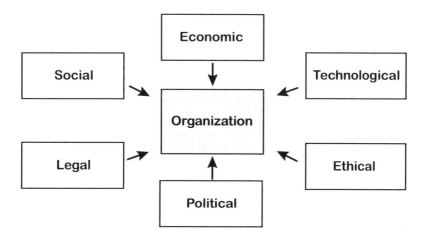

The operations of any organization whether domestic or international depend largely on these externals, which act as a constraining influence. In an international organization the impact of external influences is even more rigorous. A person deputed from a parent country to a host country has to be knowledgeable about the host country's economical, political, legal, educational, social and cultural environment.

Additionally, the management of an international company has to spend a lot of time in determining the orientation of management best suited to the host country. A birds-eye view of management orientation is represented by:

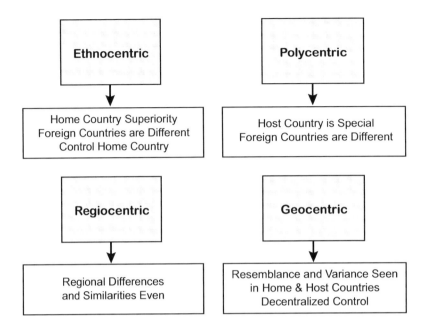

Economic Environment: Deals with the availability of capital, rate of interest, labor availability and how well they are organized, general price levels, the degree of productivity, the willingness of entrepreneurs and availability of Managerial skills.

Technological Environment: How good the available knowledge is used through technology is a factor to reckon with. How to conceive ideas, how to design, how to produce optimally, how to effect efficient distribution and how well marketing is done, are all questions that are technology-oriented.

Social Environment: It is the value systems unique to a particular group of people or society. The value system consists of attitudes, behavioral pattern, needs, wants, expectations, level of education, the degree of intelligence, general beliefs, customs and traditions followed by a particular group of people or society.

Political and Legal Environment: This consists mainly of laws, rules, regulations, governmental policies, etc., that directly affect an organization. Managers are to act within the laws of the land, follow the rules and regulations faithfully, and in case of a change in policy that has a direct bearing on the enterprise, to act accordingly.

Ethical Environment: Longman Advanced American Dictionary describes (1) "Ethics" and (2) "Ethical" as: (1) "...the study of the moral rules and principles of behavior in society, and how they influence the choices people make...," and (2) "...relating to principles of what is right and what is wrong...." Ethical Environment therefore means holding on to moral principles, guided by value systems prevalent in society and generally behaving in a responsible way.

Social Responsibilities: Organizations as well as managers should be socially responsive to the society as a whole and should be able to do their bit when a situation calls for it. They should be seen as contributing members of solutions to the social problems.

 Economic Issues

Economics is the study of how people choose to use limited resources to satisfy people's unlimited wants. Social responsibility is the idea that a business is part of something bigger than itself. It is part of a global community. With that knowledge comes the responsibility to do what is best for the company and for society as well. Some of the ways that companies can contribute to society are making environmentally friendly choices as well as contributing to charities.

There are four factors of production:

1. labor – the human resource, brain and brawn
2. land – includes all natural resources
3. capital – funds provided by investors and profits created
4. entrepreneurship – the processes of bringing the other factors together to create a good or service and a profit

Socialism is an economic system. Unlike capitalism, the government does the economic planning, owns most of the basic industries, controls the large industries and has a heavy tax to finance the welfare programs of the nation. Typical industries owned by a socialist government include coal mining, banking, major transportation like air, rail, etc. Some current social democracies include: Great Britain, Italy, Sweden, France and Austria. Under this system, the country supplies medical care, dental care, and college education.

Functional Management – Basics

Generally speaking, good managers need to possess three different qualities: technical skills, interpersonal skills and conceptual skills. Technical skills are field or task related. For example, if the job requires use of a specific computer program or piece of machinery, the manager should know how to operate it. Interpersonal skills relate to how well the manager works with other people. Good managers should be able to communicate with and inspire their employees. If they are uncommunicative or inefficient they will not be an effective manager. The third quality is conceptual skills. Conceptual skills relate to a manager's ability to identify important information, visualize and be innovative.

PLANNING

Planning comprises of setting objectives i.e., goals for the organization as well as developing work-maps that identify the ways and means of achieving such objectives. It is the most basic function of managing and all other functions are built, brick by brick, over it. Broadly speaking it revolves around the selection of not only the total organizational objectives, but departmental, even sectional goals, and more importantly spelling out in clear terms the ways through which such objectives, goals are to be accomplished.

What? How? When and Who? is decided in advance at the planning stage. What to do, How to do, When to do and Who exactly will do is the primary objective of good planning. It, therefore, precedes all other managerial functions. Since planning and controlling are related most intricately they become inseparable and therefore, a good plan always spells out yardsticks for accomplishing the planned objective. It is obvious control measures are also part and parcel of a well thought out plan.

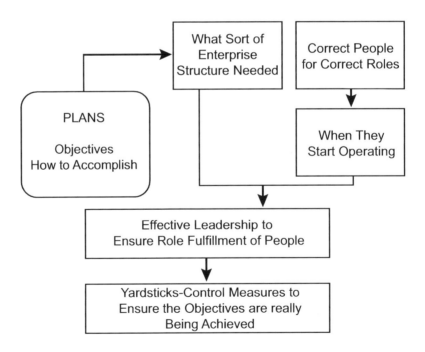

TYPES OF PLANS

What is the main purpose of the company? The purpose of a University is primarily teaching and then doing research on studies. Every organization's principal planning document gives its mission statement explaining what the organization stands for and what its activities are going to be. Example: The mission statement of Du Pont has been spelled out as "…better living through chemistry…"

Objectives are identified goals of an organization towards accomplishment of which all organizational activities are directed. It is an action program specifying what should be achieved over a specified time and what resources are to be employed in achieving such objectives.

What is an organization going to do in terms of business, i.e., what business it is aiming at and how it is going about it? What is the time frame, what are the resources and where from they are coming, who all are going to be responsible and who all are accountable for achieving the spelled out objectives? These points are to be clearly considered.

A policy can be defined as a predetermined action course that serves as a guide for the identified and accepted objectives and goals. A policy indicates the management strategy towards attainment of the overall objectives and goals and seeks to establish a platform of guiding principles, which makes delegation of work to lower levels easy.

The statement "you can delegate authority but not responsibility" is very applicable to a management setting. Managers and supervisors have the right to delegate assignments and projects to other people. They give them the authority to act to get things done. However, ultimate responsibility will always lie with them.

In order to handle future activities one needs a plan that shows clearly what methods are to be used. And this plan that establishes such methods is known as procedure. Procedures are available at every level of an organization. It is more widely adhered to in the lower levels. Some organizations have even departmental procedures cogently spelled out for the people of the department to follow. Rules give us distinct action plans without permitting any sort of discretion whatsoever. The action plan may spell out what action or non-action to be taken in clear terms. They are very simple plans.

Programs contain a simple, complicated or complex plan of activities developed primarily for carrying out stated policies. It simplifies the process of decision-making. A program generally consists of objectives, policies, procedures, rules, individual task allocations, what action or inaction to be taken or not taken by whom and when, and what resources are to be employed in order to successfully carry out a specified goal. Programs are also assisted by appropriate budgets in quantity or dollar terms.

Budgets are statements of targeted results reduced to quantifiable terms. An operating budget is a "profit plan." A territory budget spells out what the target is for the territory in terms of dollars and what will be the total resources to be spent in order to achieve that quantified (in dollar terms) target. A budget is seen as a tool of control. If an organization has variable output levels, they normally have flexible/variable budgets.

STEPS IN PLANNING

1. Analysis of Opportunities: Thorough knowledge of the plus points of your company and the products, market knowledge, knowledge on competition and knowledge as to what exactly the needs and aspirations of the customer are in so far as the products are concerned.

2. Setting of Objectives: An unambiguous objective that spells out clearly where the organization is at the moment and why, where it should be heading, what should be the best direction to get there, what specific action should be taken by whom and when, and what measures should be watched to get information on whether the plan is going on the right track and at the right speed.

3. To identify the basis: The plan has to work in what sort of environment – both external and internal. To take note of all factors that form part of the external environment.

4. To identify, analyze, compare and choose the best of available alternatives.

5. To design relevant plans that are supportive in nature such as purchasing capital goods, purchasing materials, sub-assemblies and components, recruit, train and place needed personnel, etc.

6. Quantify for control: reduce your actions into numbers – in other words work out budgets. Example: volume of business both in quantity and dollar terms for the targeted period, inventory, operating expenses, expenditure on capital goods, sales territory budgets, etc.

There are long term plans such as a 10 year or a 5 year plan which reflects the continuity of policy and short term plans like an annual plan that sets targets for the year to be achieved and which, for the sake of control, is further bifurcated into half yearly, quarterly and even monthly plans.

DECISION MAKING

The central pith, the core of planning is decision making. There are alternatives available. Choosing the best alternative from a plethora of available alternatives and sticking to it is the focus of decision making.

In decision-making you have to identify the <u>Limiting Factor</u>, which can be defined as something, which stands in the way of achieving a goal. The impediment. Identify the limiting factor or factors and solve them in order to arrive at the best possible decision. How to evaluate alternatives? There are Marginal Analysis Models and Cost-effective Analysis Models. The Marginal Analysis deals in analyzing the additional units of revenue one gets from incurring a certain unit of additional costs. The cost-effective analysis deals in cost-benefit analysis, i.e., the ratio of benefits to costs. Your experience, ability to experiment and an analytical bent of mind helps you to arrive at a rational decision under specific given circumstances. <u>Operations Research</u> lends a scientific aura to management decision-making. There are goals, models, variables, limitations – all such factors are built into quantifiable mathematical terms or formulae to decipher and arrive at the best decision possible under a given circumstance. Not all the managers are equipped mathematically to decide among alternative solutions. It is sometimes difficult to quantify a factor. In such cases operations research can do little about it. There is <u>Risk Analysis</u>, which again is a method steeped in mathematical terms – it tells you what probabilities are there to arrive at decisional outcomes. There are <u>Decision Trees</u>, which again are statistical models which tell us which are the possible decision points, chance events which are likely to occur and what probabilities are there for each course of action. Then there is Preference Theory, which tells you a given manager's willingness to take or refrain from taking (unwillingness) risks.

The bounded rationality model is another decision-making model. This model is based on the theory that people will try to find the answer to their problem, but will settle for a less than perfect solution because it involves more work than they bargained for.

The model was developed by Herbert Simon. He developed it in response to and as a criticism of the rationality model. Simon believed that there were three steps in problem solving. First the decision maker must decide if there is a legitimate problem. This is called the intelligence stage. It may involve talking with workers, going over budget and profit summaries, monitoring the workplace, or any other sort of action which helps them gather information about the problem. Second, the decision maker develops a list of possible solutions. This is called the design stage. For example, if a company is not bringing in enough profit, the decision maker may consider raising product price, laying of a number of employees, or cutting production or distribution costs. In the final step the decision maker will "satisfice." Simon gave the step this unique name because it involves a combination of satisfying the problem, and sacrificing the best solution for one which is "good enough."

The SWOT analysis method takes a view of both internal and external factors to analyze the success of a business. SWOT stands for Strengths (advantageous internal characteristics), Weaknesses (harmful internal characteristics), Opportunities (advantageous external factors) and Threats (harmful external factors). On the other hand, the Upstream Capital Costs Index (UCCI) tracks costs of equipment, facilities, materials and personnel for a number of large companies. This offers a benchmark or comparison for other companies to look to and compare their own business to. Both methods can be helpful in considering and analyzing the resources needed for a company to be successful.

CHANGE

Change is the essence of life. There are different levels of changes.

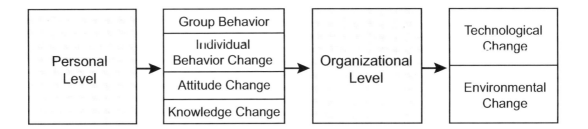

At the personal level knowledge changes are the easiest. Once you read this book you will have gained a little more knowledge than you had before starting it. Attitudinal change is not as difficult as individual behavior change, though time and conscious effort is needed. Group behavior change is a little more difficult than individual behavior change. Group behavior change affects an organization.

If people as a group within an organization demand certain things, say, increased rest periods, lesser number of work hours, it impacts the organization and the Personnel Manager has to deal with such a situation. At organizational level, environmental changes – Social, Economic, Political, Legal – any change in any of the components, is going to affect the organization adversely. In the case of technological change, an organization has to face the music, if it does not adapt itself to the changes adeptly and with speed. A change is certainly a limiting factor in the planning process.

Rapid changes more especially in the environmental and technological areas impact organizational plans adversely. In the field of computers, the chip capacity of the hard disks increased in breathtaking speed. A 2-gigabyte hard disk is considered obsolete

– as there are 1 TB hard disks available. Again the increase in speed of chips is breathtaking! Once radios used bulky, noisy, inelegant, vacuum tubes, which became obsolete after Bell laboratories designed transistors. In such rapidly changing, highly competitive environment, it is your own creativity and techniques bordering on innovation that are necessary to exist. Fast adaptability to change is the key.

Kurt Lewin identified three stages of change. They are:

- Unfreeze
- Transition
- Refreeze

People feel comfortable and sage when they feel a sense of control and understand their role in the community and their environment. They attach their identity to their environment, so any changes, even those that are positive and will offer real benefits cause discomfort. Because of this discomfort, talking about future changes is not enough to move the average person from the frozen state and a lot of effort may be needed to unfreeze them and get them going. When people are unfrozen and ready to take the next step, they are referred to as change ready.

Lewin's model says that change is a journey and not just a simple step. There may be multiple small changes that result in getting to where they (or the organization) want them to be. A failling for managers implementing these changes is the expectation to have everyone on the team get to the end result in just one change.

Transitions take time and managers need to adjust their expectations to be in line.

Once the changes are made, a refreeze is in order, to establish the new reality and make it permanent. Refreezing may be slow as the transitions continue to be in a state of flux. Sometimes this results in a slushy environment, where the company is constantly changing, but slowly enough that it is at least a bit frozen.

ORGANIZING

Organizing defines organizational roles to be played by individuals, their positions and the authority relationships. Every role should be clearly defined with distinct objectives in mind. The major duties to be performed by individuals, how responsibilities are to be delegated and with what authority are to be included in the organizing process. Should also indicate what resources are available, what information and tools are necessary to carry out such roles effectively. This is organizing in a nutshell. A formal organization is what we have seen above. An informal organization according to Chester Barnard is any joint personal activity without conscious joint purpose, even though possibly contributing to joint results. The relationships in an informal organization never reflect in any organizational chart. There may be sub-assembly groups, stress groups or accounts groups, i.e., groups of individuals. However, each group identifies itself as a contributing member and acts in unison where the group's ideal or any given member's identity or right is challenged.

ORGANIZATIONAL THEORIES

Many theorists propounded a number of theories of which the following three are important: (1) Classical Organization Theory, (2) The Mechanistic Theory, and (3) The System Theory. The <u>Classical Organizational Theory</u> deals in specializing job assignments, works towards easy managerial functions, seeks to establish authority structures and delegation of responsibility and authority, maintains bureaucracy which speaks of offices and roles and institutes formal channels of communication among members of different departments in the organization. It deals in division of labor, vertical and horizontal specialization, scalar authority, etc.

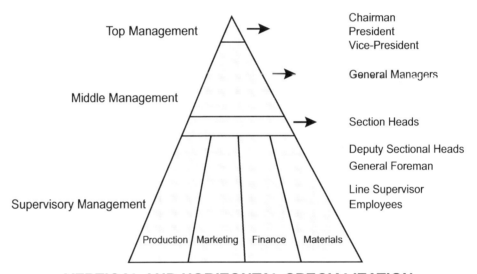

VERTICAL AND HORIZONTAL SPECIALIZATION

The <u>Mechanistic Theory</u> states that organizational change is inevitable and that organizations and people within the organizations have no other choice except following natural law. Industrialization brought in its wake a laissez faire philosophy in political circles, which advocated the integrity or virtue of letting the natural process take its own course.

This theory was supported by economic philosophy prevalent at that time. In a way it is a precursor to the later scientific management movement. The theorists had foreseen the potency of competition. They thought specialization was a tool for obtaining competitive advantage. The later versions of this theory harp on compensation structures. Both the classical organizational and the Mechanistic theories took people for granted.

This gradually created uncertainties in the minds of workers and opposition started. This situation necessitated bringing focus on people. Unions and collective bargaining showed their head. Human relations principles were born out of necessity. The Systems Theory deals with interdependence instead of independence of variables and their interactions. It started with a more intensive, very broad, wide-angle – involving a number of variables to measure complex inter-relationships – and inclusive viewpoint.

Group behavior is seen in the system as broadly shaped and influenced. There are various elements in an organizational system but the common choice of an element is the individual in an organization. It identifies the system as changing, evolving and most dynamic. The systems model recognizes the environment of the system and other related variables, which includes all other subsystems and seeks to elucidate an adequate explanation of organizational behavior. The system as a whole is seen as an open system.

ORGANIZATIONAL STRUCTURES

Any formal organization can be described as an intentional structure of roles. For the sake of functionality, a formal organizational structure is divided into many departments on the basis of their functions. There may be an Accounts department, a Marketing department, a Production department, a Material department, an Engineering department and so on.

A department typically has a Head or Boss followed by a Deputy and then the assisting employees. In such a scenario, the roles of the Department Head, the Deputy and the assisting employees should be very clear and the authority relationship should be spelled out. The cooperation of all the people making up a department should be effective in order to achieve the overall organizational objectives. How many people can a department head or his deputy effectively control is the crux of the "Span" of management. There are two types – (1) Narrow Span, and (2) Wide Span.

Structure
An Organization with a Narrow Span

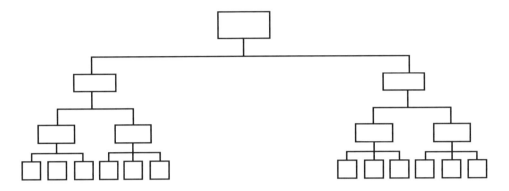

Structure
An Organization with a Wide Span

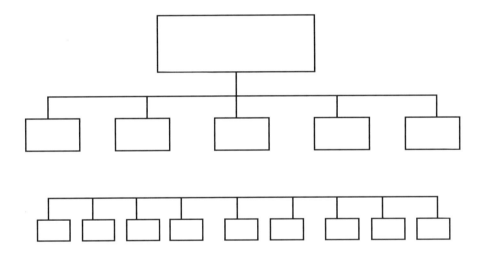

In a narrow span organizational structure, close supervision is possible, good control, and communication between Department Head and subordinates occur quickly. The disadvantage is that the super is closely involved in the subordinate's work – delegation is missing. There are many levels of management necessitating increased cost to the organization.

In a broad span organizational structure delegation becomes essential. There is a possibility of a superior losing control of subordinates. Managerial effectiveness dictates placing high quality managers. Delegation of responsibility along with requisite authority is the crux of broad span organizational structure.

AUTHORITY

In order to achieve company objectives and to sail smoothly on the chosen direction towards that objective, the superiors need authority to enforce compliance of company policies, procedures and rules by subordinates. 'Scalar' authority is identified with rank, position as well as title.

LINE AND STAFF AUTHORITY

They are identified with relationships and not departments. In Line Authority a superior is directly responsible for the organizational actions of a subordinate. It entails making decisions and acting upon them. In Staff Authority it is limited only to the extent of giving counsel/advice. The advice given by Staff Authority is not binding on Line Authority.

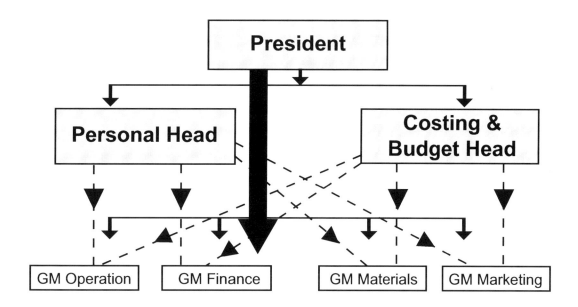

LINE AND FUNCTIONAL AUTHORITY

Functional authority is the right of people in other departments (i.e., other than one's own) to control selected policies, practices, procedures, processes or other functional matters with the sole aim of accomplishing set organizational goals.

A flat organization is an organization with no mid level management. In this format, the top level management comes into direct contact with the low level employees. This can be beneficial when a company needs to have a fast response time to changes in markets. However, it is not always feasible when a company is large.

DELEGATION OF AUTHORITY

The idea behind delegation is to make organizing easy. A collective effort is the key to success in an organization. Delegation of authority happens when a super-ordinate bestows on a subordinate discretion to make decisions in the best interest of the organization. It can be specific to perform a task or a cluster of tasks, or general, written or unwritten. It is also possible for the super-ordinate to revoke the delegated authority any time.

UNITY OF COMMAND

The reporting relationship of a subordinate will be smooth and effective if it is to a single superior. If an employee has to report to more than one superior then confusion, inefficiency, lack of control and total chaos prevail. A subordinate reporting to a single superior is unity of command in its simplest definition.

CENTRALIZATION AND DECENTRALIZATION

In centralization all authority is concentrated at the top. In decentralization, decision making is widely dispersed. A decentralized authority, if it is re-centralized or to put it simply, if all the authority dispersed is revoked and centralized again, it is called re-centralization of authority.

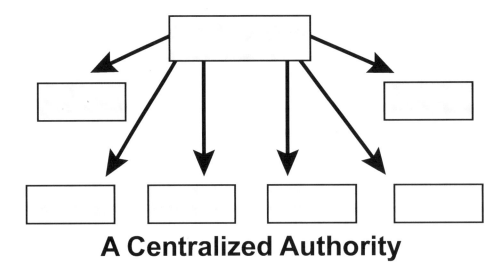

A Centralized Authority

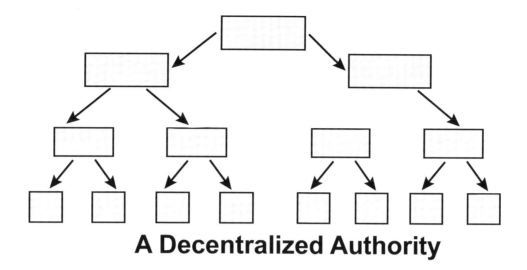

A Decentralized Authority

ORGANIZATION CHARTS

Functional grouping of a manufacturing organization

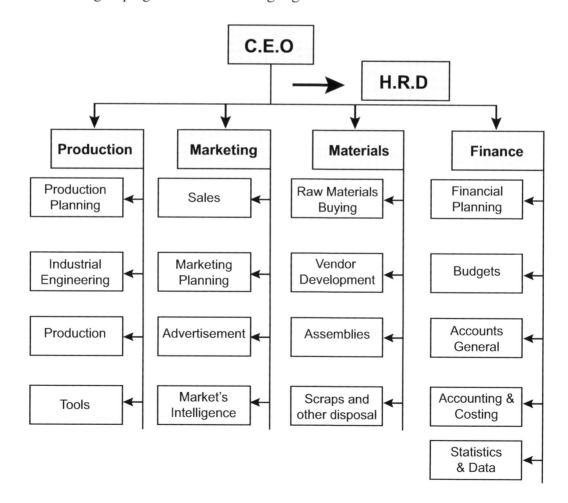

Territorial grouping of a manufacturing organization

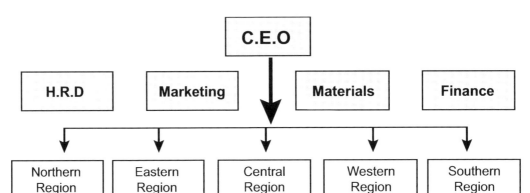

Market-oriented grouping of an organization

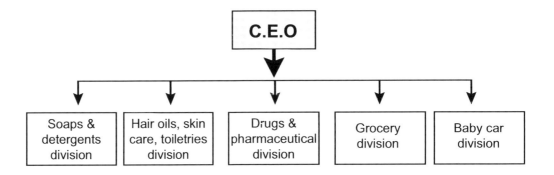

STAFFING

In organizing we have seen authority structures, broad departmentalization, delegation, etc. In other words we have a structure and we need people to fill up the structures to do meaningful jobs. Staffing, therefore, is a systematic and methodical filling up of positions in an organizational structure by identifying total manpower requirements, recruitment, selection, placement, appraisal, promotion, training and compensation. Organizing and staffing are closely linked.

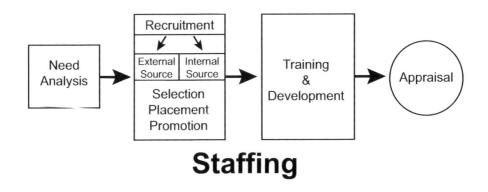

Staffing

DIRECTING

Directing = Leadership + Motivation + Communication. Directing is the process, which seeks to influence people towards spontaneous and willing accomplishment of overall organizational objectives. Let us consider the components of Directing.

LEADERSHIP

Peter F. Drucker, the Modern Management philosopher and guru states in his book "The Practice of Management" "...The successful organization has one major attribute that sets it apart from unsuccessful organizations: dynamic and effective leadership..." Again, George R Terry, in his wonderful book "Principles of Management" points out that: "...Of every one hundred new business establishments started, approximately fifty, or one half, go out of business within two years. By the end of five years, only one third of the original one hundred will still be in business..." Almost all the failures were attributed to <u>ineffective leadership</u>. This tells us in clear and unambiguous terms all about leadership. In other words, the core of leadership is accomplishment of goals <u>with</u> and <u>through</u> people. Every leader has a style. The style of leaders is the consistent behavior patterns that they exhibit when they seek to influence people in order to accomplish organizational goals. The style is the consistent perception of the followers/subordinates of the leader and not the leader's perception itself.

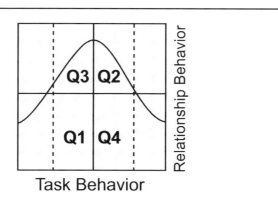

Q = Quadrant

Q1 = Telling stage where the leader perceives the subordinates maturity level as immature. Here he spells out clearly every task.

Q2 = Selling stage where the leader perceives the maturity level of his subordinates as moderate. Here he just gives what is expected and he would like the task done.

Q3 = Participating stage where the leader perceives the subordinate to be fairly matured and invites him to participate in decisions.

Q4 = Delegating stage were the leader thinks that the subordinate to be fully matured to take on responsibilities. He only gives a broad outline and leaves the execution to the subordinate.

There are despotic leaders who only demand what they want normally in high decibels, and encourage no initiative. They are task leaders. On the other side of the spectrum you have leaders who value human relationships, who are polite but firm with subordinates, encourage initiative and are willing to share responsibilities.

Many leaders **empower** their employees by allowing them to make their own decisions and / or giving them authorization to do certain behaviors to help a customer.

There are several different types of leaders:

- **Laissez Faire Leadership** is a hands-off approach. Employees are highly motivated and complete their tasks without a lot of input or supervision.

- **Autocratic Leadership** is the dictator approach. Employees are told who, what, how, where and when. Also known as the "because I said so" style of leadership.

- **Participative Leadership** is where the leader asks for and considers input from their employees for decision making.

- **Situational Leadership** is when a leader chooses the best style for the situation varying between all shades of different approaches.

MOTIVATION

William James of Harvard University did a research on Motivation. His findings are noteworthy. He found that hourly employees whose work pattern he studied could hold on to their jobs, if they performed at 20 to 30% of their ability. His studies further elucidated that workmen can work up to 80 to 90% of their ability if they are highly motivated! In other words if the employees are highly motivated their work ability jumps from 20-30% to 80-90%!

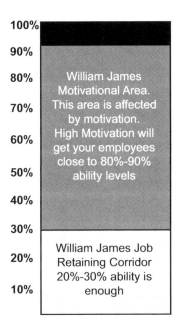

For some money can be a good motivator. For some others safety, i.e., security, job-satisfaction, congenial atmosphere, social needs, esteem needs and self-actualization needs are important. Challenge in one's job is a motivation for some people. Rewards for accomplishments are also a motivator.

Frederick Herzberg developed a theory of motivation called the two factor model. To do this he asked people about times when they had strong positive and strong negative feelings about their jobs. According to Herzberg, there were two different types of factors which influence job satisfaction. They are hygiene factors and motivational factors. Herzberg's theory is unique because he believed that the absence of hygiene factors caused dissatisfaction, but that introducing them wouldn't create satisfaction, only eliminate dissatisfaction.

On the other hand, he believed that the presence of motivational factors caused job satisfaction, whereas their absence, rather than creating dissatisfaction, created neutrality. In other words Herzberg believed that the two factors, and thus satisfaction and dissatisfaction, operate entirely independent of one other.

Hygiene factors are things which relate to the actual environment. This includes cleanliness, benefits, work policies, status, and even salary. On the opposite end, motivational factors include level of responsibility, feelings of accomplishment, recognition, available opportunities, and the work itself.

To put it in context, according to Herzberg, employees become unhappy if the environment is unclean, but a cleaner environment won't make them more satisfied. Also, employees are happy when they are given responsibilities, receive encouragement and feelings of accomplishment, however the absence of these factors won't make them upset.

Clayton P. Alderfer developed a theory of motivation that focused on three levels of needs. The theory, called the **ERG theory,** focuses on the needs of existence, relatedness, and growth. Alderfer specifically related his model to people and their job situations. The existence level focuses on needs related to physical well being. Benefit plans, food, housing, and salary are all considered existence needs.

The second level, relatedness, has to do with emotional needs such as feelings of belonging and love, which is equated in the working world as the strength of interpersonal relations, frequency of company activities, and breaks. The highest level, growth, refers to needs such as self esteem, responsibility, status, and challenge. Although the theory contains levels, the progression is not step-by-step. A person will focus on the area which they lack the most.

Contingency Leadership

The idea that different situations call for different leadership styles is called the contingency theory. According to the contingency theory, while some types of work require an upbeat and positive manager or leader, others are more effective when a strict and regulatory leader is present. This is called contingency leadership, or in other words, it is the theory that a leader's style should suit the situation as well as the task.

One of the first contingency theories was developed by Fred Fiedler. Fiedler believed that a leader's style should change based on the leader's personality and the impending situation. His model addressed three different issues, leader-member relations, task structure, and leader power. He believed that various arrangements of these three factors would require either task motivated leaders or relationship motivated leaders.

Leader-member relations can be good or poor and refer to the extent to which the group accepts the leader. This is also determined using what Fielder called the LPC, or the least preferred coworker. If a leader's least preferred coworker was described positively, it indicated good leader-member relations and a relationship motivated style. If the leader's least preferred coworker was described negatively, it indicated poor leader-member relations and a task motivated style.

Task structure can be described as structured or unstructured. This is the extent to which a task must be done a certain way, or if the task is flexible or requires creativity. For example, an industrial worker must always produce a product in the exact same way, whereas a computer company needs to continually work on new and different products. The industrial worker is structured and the computer company is unstructured.

The final element, leader power, can be either strong or weak and describes the extent to which the leader exercises power over the employees. An example of this power would be the ability to hire, fire, and promote employees. The three elements in various combinations create either high control, moderate control, or low control situations. According to Fiedler, high and low control situations require a task motivated leader. Moderate control situations require a relationship motivated leader.

The contingency theory of leadership says that there is not one single perfect way to lead a group, but that the style of leadership should change based on the situation. Fred Fiedler believes that a leader's style should change based on the leader's personality and the impending situation.

There are three factors that influence the favorableness of a leader:

1. Leader-member relations
2. Task structure
3. Leader position power

When each of these three areas is rated highly, the situation is considered a favorable situation.

 **Path-Goal Model**

A second contingency theory is called the path-goal model. This model was developed mainly by Robert House, and states that the job of a leader is to use structure, support, and rewards to create a good working environment which encourages accomplishing the organization's goals. The leader should be able to show the workers how accomplishing the company's goals will benefit them. The leader should also provide for task needs, such as supplies and budgets, and psychological support, such as encouragement.

Leaders may choose between four different styles, and the choice should be based on considerations of the worker's opinions and styles, and the work environment. The leadership styles are directive, supportive, participative and achievement-oriented.

In directive leadership, the leader clearly outlines what the workers are to do and accomplish, and how they are to do so. They provide standards, schedules, and instructions. For ambiguous or difficult tasks, this style of leadership can be appreciated and helpful.

Supportive leadership involves an open approach, with considerate and helpful leaders. The leaders create a pleasing work environment and look after the workers. This style is helpful in the situation of a tedious, unpleasant, or stressful job. If a job is repetitive, supportive leadership increases job satisfaction among workers. Participative leadership involves a group oriented structure. The leader asks the worker's opinions and considers their input. This style of leadership is most effective in nonrepetitive tasks. For example, a worker who watches an assembly line all day will appreciate being asked for their opinions much less than a lawyer, who has continually changing goals, or a person feels challenged by their job.

Achievement-oriented leadership involves a pattern of high goal setting and encouragement. This style involves challenging workers, and expressing confidence in their abilities. This style of leadership is most effective in ambiguous and challenging situations, and not for repetitive or simple tasks.

The path-goal theory leaders make it easy for subordinates to meet their goals. They:

- Provide a clear path
- Help remove barriers to the problems
- Increase the rewards along and at the end of the route

Situational leadership focuses on three main points:

1. the amount of leadership direction to subordinates
2. the amount of monetary support for goals
3. the willingness of subordinates to perform

Vroom and Yetton's normative leadership model is used in decision-making. This model helps leaders determine when and how much feedback from a group is required when making a decision. Who makes the decisions is factored heavily into the supervisor's leadership style. This theory states that no one leadership style or decision making process fits all situations equally.

Power in the workplace is known as a person's ability to influence peers, subordinates and events. Power is earned not by title but by a person on their own. Politics is the way that a person gains power. Politics include bargaining, negotiating, compromises, etc. To succeed in a corporate structure, you must have a skill for politics.

Some people have referent power which is also called charisma. Legitimate power is obtained through a specific position in the organization by a title. Legitimate power is the right to fire and hire others. Expert power is when someone is an expert at a certain task or in a certain area. Although that person may not have subordinates, they have power because of their expertise. For example, a web designer may have power if they are the only one in the organization that can provide for a web design need.

 Vroom-Yetton Model

A third contingency model is called the Vroom-Yetton model, or Vroom-Yetton normative leadership model. This model follows the belief that every decision that a leader must make requires a different approach, each with a different level of involvement from subordinates, and it therefore follows a decision tree structure.

Using the model, the leader will consider a series of questions that will lead them to styles which incorporate different levels of autocratic, consultative, and group properties. There are two levels of autocratic procedures. The autocratic procedures involve decisions made by the leader, with little or no involvement from subordinates. The first autocratic level, AI, is when the leader makes the decision completely on their own using only the information which is currently available to them, or things which they already know.

For example, a leader must decide how to increase profit, and they decide that they are going to fire one of the employees they don't know with very well. They don't consult anyone, and just make the decision themselves based on the fact that they don't know the person.

The second autocratic level, AII, involves the leader gathering specific information from others, and making the choice by themselves. For example, if the same leader is determining which employee to fire, they may ask a number of employees which person is the worst worker. Often with the AII level, the leader may not even tell the people they ask what the specific problem is.

They still make the choice on their own, and may completely disregard the information they gather, but they do ask. There are also two levels of consultative procedure. In this case, the decision is made by the leader, but there is involvement from the subordinates.

The first level, CI, involves sharing the problem with individual employees and asking their opinions one at a time, never as a group. Then the decision is made. The second level, CII, involves gathering all the employees into a group and allowing discussion. In this way, the leader determines the opinion of the group and receives ideas and suggestions from them. The leader will make the decision based on what they say. The decision still may not agree with what the subordinates say.

There is one level of group involvement, GII. This level involves sharing the problem with the subordinates as a group and allowing them to choose a solution to the problem. When it is important that the subordinates support the decision which is made, or if the subordinates have relevant information to contribute, the autocratic methods are not very useful. However, if the subordinates do not see the problem as important or relevant, and the leader does, the autocratic methods are the most useful. It all depends on the specific situation.

Victor Vroom's expectancy theory is a model for determining the motivation of an employee. It relies on the strength of three factors: expectancy, instrumentality and valence. Expectancy is if an employee believes a task to be possible. This is measured as one if they believe it to be possible, zero if they do not believe it to be possible and anywhere in between if think believe it might be possible.

Valency is the extent to which the employee believes that the task will produce a positive outcome or a negative outcome. It is measured on a scale from one (if positive) to negative one (if negative).

Instrumentality is the probability that completing the task will lead to the desired outcome. The employees motivation can be determined by multiplying the three values together. For example, if an employee is assigned a task and they have an expectancy of .5, a valency of 1 and an instrumentality of .5, then they believe the task may or may not be possible, and there is a fifty-fifty chance that it will produce a very positive outcome. In this situation, their motivation is .25.

Lifecycle Model

Another contingency model is called the lifecycle model, or the Hersey and Blanchard situational leadership model. The lifecycle model has its main focus on the state of the worker. The worker has high readiness if they are able and very willing to accomplish a task. Conversely, a worker has low readiness if there are incapable, inept, or unwilling to accomplish a task.

By incorporating their task behavior and relationship behavior, or the extent to which the leader is involved in the task and how the leader communicates, it states four different leadership types. If a leader has high task behavior and high relationship behavior, it is called a selling style. This style involves explaining decisions, and persuading workers.

The selling style is best used in the case where workers have moderate readiness. In this style, it is primarily the leader who makes decisions after discussion with the workers. If a leader has high task behavior and low relationship behavior it is called a telling style. This style primarily involves close supervision and extensive instruction. This style is best used when there is a very low level of readiness, such as when workers are unwilling or insecure.

If a leader has low task behavior and high relationship behavior it is called a participating style. This style involves group decisions, in which the leader collaborates and encourages the workers. This style is best used in the case of moderate to high levels of readiness.

The final style is delegating. In a delegating style, the leader has low task behavior and low relationship behavior. The leader will give out assignments to the workers and allow them to function for themselves. This style is best used in the case of high readiness, because it allows the competent and willing workers to accomplish tasks as they wish.

Each of the four styles has a distinct view, however they are all considered contingency models because they accept the premise that there is not a single type of leader, or leadership style, which works best in every situation. They all combine different aspects including work environment, purpose, and leader personality to provide models describing the type of leadership which they believe would best suit the specific situation.

Vertical-Dyad Linkages

Vertical-dyad linkage is also called leader-member exchange or LMX. Vertical refers to the chain of command, the relationship between leaders and subordinates, and a dyad is a group of two people. Therefore, vertical-dyad linkages are relationships between a leader and worker. In layman's terms this could be referred to as favoritism. Simply put, vertical-dyad linkages occur when a leader and a follower have mutual respect, trust and obligation towards each other.

Essentially vertical-dyad linkages are friendships which cause the development of in-groups and out-groups in a working environment. The in-groups receive favorable treatment such as interesting assignments, promotions and raises. The out-groups are the groups which do not share the mutual respect and obligations of a vertical-dyad linkage, and therefore are at a disadvantage. In-group workers tend to be more productive and enthusiastic. On the other hand, when the gap between treatment of in-group and out-groups becomes too large it can become a problem. Out-groups may become resentful or angry, and therefore less productive.

 Motivation

William James of Harvard University did a research on Motivation. His findings are noteworthy. He found that hourly employees whose work pattern he studied could hold on to their jobs, if they performed at 20 to 30% of their ability. His studies further elucidated that workmen can work up to 80 to 90% of their ability if they are highly motivated! In other words if the employees are highly motivated their work ability jumps from 20-30% to 80-90%!

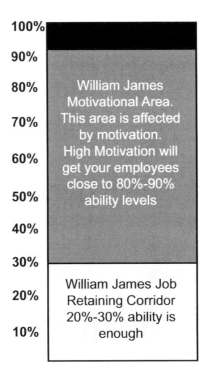

For some money can be a good motivator. For some others safety, i.e., security, job-satisfaction, congenial atmosphere, social needs, esteem needs and self-actualization needs are important. Challenge in one's job is a motivation for some people. Rewards for accomplishments are also a motivator.

COMMUNICATION

In communication there is a sender and a receiver. If the sender sends information (message) to the receiver and if the information is understood in full by the receiver, you have communicated successfully. The main purpose of communication in an organizational setting is to influence action aimed at achieving the common goals of the organization.

Communication is a very important factor in effective leadership and management. Not only the leaders (superiors) but also the followers (subordinates) should be adept in communicating.

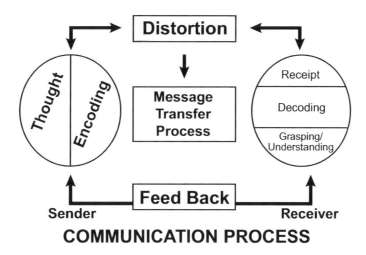

COMMUNICATION PROCESS

In an organization there are upward and downward communication, horizontal communication and diagonal communication.

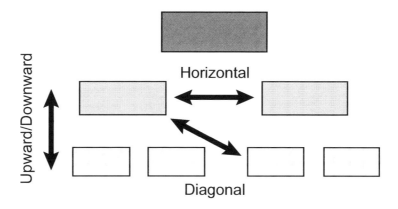

COMMUNICATION/INFORMATION FLOW IN AN ORGANIZATIONAL SETTING

Communication can be oral, written or non-verbal. When a message is repeated through various media, the comprehension and recall of that message is high with the receiver of such message. Simple words, using personal pronouns, adding graphs or graphics, short sentenced paragraphs, logical, cohesive and cogent presentation, and avoiding verborrhea will ensure good communication.

GROUP DYNAMICS

It is one of the training techniques used in organizations. Group dynamics deals with role playing coupled with simulation which seeks to emphasize group behavior, how groups influence decision making and how inter-group rivalry or conflicts affect organizational effectiveness. Participants discuss team development, team member hygiene, issues that are construed as disruptive and team health.

PROBLEM SOLVING

Of all the skills a manager is expected to possess, analytical and problem solving abilities are most important. There are broadly three skills associated with managing. They are: (1) Conceptual skills, (2) Human relation skills, and (3) Technical skills.

For all the levels – Top, Middle and Supervisory – the emphasis is Human skills. "...I will pay more for the ability to deal with people than any other ability under the sun..." said John D. Rockefeller, one of the great American entrepreneurs. Managers should be ever vigilant to identify problems as they arise, analyze and track the core issue and then solve the problem by addressing the core issue and exploiting the opportunities present. After all opportunities are always there in every possible threat.

CONFLICT RESOLUTION

Ask yourself, what is the conflict all about? What are the causes of the conflict? What are the possible solutions? And, what is the best of the possible solutions? Is the solution acceptable to all? Yes means you have resolved the conflict.

In an organizational backdrop, if the individual and group goals are seen as close to the organizational goals, there is bound to be an integration of goals, which satisfies all concerned.

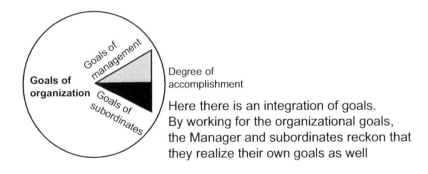

Degree of accomplishment

Here there is an integration of goals. By working for the organizational goals, the Manager and subordinates reckon that they realize their own goals as well

In psychological terms conflict arises when frustration develops. The blocking or stymieing of goal accomplishment is known as frustration. In an organization conflicts arise mainly because the people in the organization have not understood their roles, assignments, tasks as well as those of their co-workers. You can educate people by having proper organization charts, authority structures, clear-cut job descriptions and job specifications, together with specific goals. Job enrichment and job rotation are also helpful.

CONTROLLING

In every organization, the top management sets out the overall company objectives, departmental targets, etc., for the managers and their team of people to accomplish during a given period of time. Managers use many tools to ensure the targeted objectives are realized effectively and efficiently. Controlling, in its larger perspective, involves the measurement of activities of subordinates in order to know whether the organizational targets are realized as per plans and if there happens to be a lagging behind, what corrective actions are to be taken to ensure 100% achievement. There are four elements in a control system:

MANAGEMENT BY OBJECTIVES – MBO

Introduced by Peter F. Drucker (The Practice of Management) and popularized by Messrs George Odiorne and John Humbe, this participative approach is good for goal setting as well as control. The superior and the subordinates of an organization jointly identify its common goals – this is the first step. Then they define an individual team member's major areas of responsibility, which is considered on the basis of results, expected of that individual – this is the second step. And using these measures as a sort of guide to run the organization as well as appraising the individual team member's contribution – this is the third step.

NORMAL STANDARDS IN PRACTICE

Standards fall within the following types: 1) Physical Standards, 2) Capital Standards, 3) Revenue Standards, 4) Cost Standards, 5) Intangible Standards, and 6) Goals standardized for verification.

Physical Standards: Quantified standards at the operating level. Products produced in numbers, in value, material used in weightage and value, labor employed in house and in value, services rendered in value, etc.

Capital Standards: Physical items and monetary value pertaining to the capital goods used in production.

Revenue Standards: Giving monetary values to realized sales.

Cost Standards: Monetary value for the cost of operations, such as machine-hour-costs, cost of material per unit, cost of labor per unit, cost per unit of sales, etc.

Intangible Standards: These relate to human efforts and for these, it is difficult to allot a standardized measurement value.

BUDGETS – AN IMPORTANT CONTROL TECHNIQUE

Budgets are plans for a specific future period of time given in numerical or value terms. They are anticipated results in value terms of a given plan. There are cash budgets, revenue/expense budgets, materials budgets, products budgets, capital expenditure budgets, etc.

MANAGERIAL CONTROL TOOLS (MILESTONE BUDGETS)

Gantt Charts: There are many types of Gantt charts in vogue. They may be called a particular type of bar chart and the measuring unit invariably is time. For example, a progress chart – here the planned target is compared with the actual accomplishment:

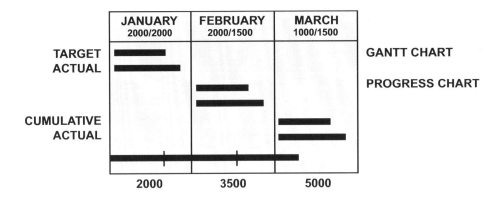

Means Chart: This is used in statistical quality control situations.

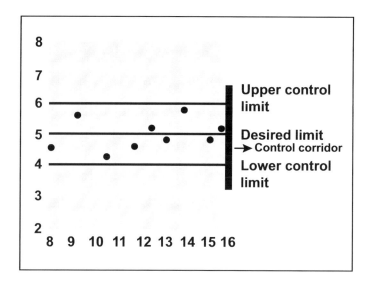

Pert (Program evaluation and review technique) and CPM (Critical Path Method):

NASA used these techniques extensively in its space programs. A project's most probable time of completion can be worked out through these techniques. Let us see an organization's budget preparation in Pert form:

Job	Description	Time Required
a	Forecasting sales	10 days
b	Market research on pricing structures of competitor	4 days
c	Sales valuing	4 days
d	Production schedules	6 days
e	Costing of production	5 days
f	Budget preparation	8 days

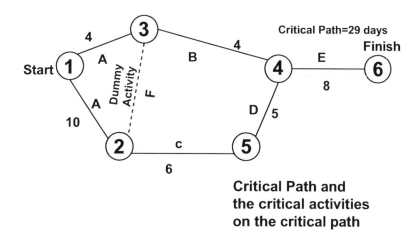

Critical Path and the critical activities on the critical path

The above is a very simple pert chart. However, such charts are prepared by giving a most pessimistic time, a most optimistic time, and a most probable time. These can then be reduced into the following formula for easy calculation.

Weightage:

t_o = optimistic time – equally likely to occur
t_p = pessimistic time – equally likely to occur
$4t_m$ = most probable time = 4 times more likely to occur than t_o, t_p.
t_e = time expected

Formula: $t_e = t_o + 4t_m + t_p / 6$

You have to arrive at standard deviation $S_t = t_p - t_o / 6$, which is one sixth of the difference between two extreme time estimates. Since standard deviation is the square root of any given distribution, we calculate variance from $V_t = (t_p - t_o / 0)2$ using probability distribution, and thus we can say expected duration of a project.

A dummy job takes only zero time for performance but it is used to show the precedence relationship. Critical path may be defined as the longest path in the network. Jobs (activities) throughout the critical paths are known as critical jobs, or critical activities.

 Human Resource Management

ABRAHAM MASLOW'S HIERARCHY OF NEEDS

Maslow's Hierarchy of Needs consists of the following stages, from the top down:

* Self-actualization
* Esteem needs
* Belonging and love
* Safety
* Physical needs

These stages begin at physical needs. First you need to have food, water, and shelter before you can worry about other things. Once those needs are met, you may start to think of other things such as safety. You might buy a gun or move to a more prosperous and safe area. Once you are fed, clothed and safe, you will want to meet needs of belonging and love through relationships. If you feel loved, you may begin to think about your self-esteem and how you feel as a person, what you are contributing. The final stage, self-actualization, you may never meet. Most people do not.

HAWTHORNE EFFECT

In 1927 a series of studies began at Western Electric Company in Hawthorne, Illinois. The first study was testing the assumption that the worker output would increase if the level of light in the plant was turned up. To test the theory, they took several female workers into a separate room in the factory and tested their output against a variety of lighting. Surprisingly, output increased regardless of the light level, until it was too dark to see and then it remained constant. Why? By taking the workers into another room at the plant, they had done something inadvertently, they had made the workers feel special. Experts coin this example to be the Hawthorne effect, which is where the interest in the people's problems affect the outcome, not the changes themselves.

THEORY X & Y

Theory X is a management approach where you believe that people dislike work and responsibility and are only motivated by money and other financial incentives. It also assumes that these people must be micro managed and supervised.

Theory Y is the assumption that all people enjoy work, and will control their own performance if you give them the chance. These people will want to do a good job and work better with a hands off approach.

PERSONNEL ADMINISTRATION

All resources in an organization need management, i.e., they are subjected to the processes of management viz., planning, organizing, directing and controlling. Building and machinery are physical resources. Stocks, bank balances are financial resources. People are human resources. While no other resource – capital, land, machines can talk back, only human resources can think and talk back and this makes management of this resource that much more difficult.

Personnel Administration is that branch of general management which: (a) looks into manpower resources of an organization (b) has a managerial function of planning, organizing, directing and controlling and an operative function of recruiting, developing, compensating, integrating human resources together with keeping records on manpower (c) aims at harmonious labor (d) aims to achieve organizational goals by integrating human resources.

The form "industrial relations" is a broader concept, which seeks to bring in harmonious relationship between labor, managements and the government of an industry.

The term "labor management" normally defines the managing of manual workers of an organization. Working conditions and worker discipline together with the general recruitment, selection, compensation, etc., are dealt with by labor management.

The scope of "personnel management" is truly wider. It deals with the recruitment, selection, placement, training, compensation, working condition, etc., pertaining to all categories of personnel in an organization. Personnel and ministration also deals with generation of mutual trust, total cooperation and cohesive work force culture and maintaining cordial relations with trade unions.

Some important terms that you will need to know:

Job analysis: the process of making a list of the exact tasks or activities that an individual in a specific job does

Job design: the ideal requirements of a job or person

Job description: a listing of what a job includes such as tasks, duties and responsibilities (analysis is the process of creating a job description)

Job relatedness: how essential job tasks are related to the job

PERFORMANCE APPRAISALS

An organization's current human resources need timely evaluation of their capabilities in order to be ready for any future needs. There are two sources where managers look to appraise capabilities of human resources. (1) Personnel records (which are built on the applications submitted), and, (2) Personnel Appraisal ratings. (1) Personnel records give all the data in the application together with high school, college and other educational institutional records, selection test scores, salary/wage started and changes made during the service, promotional opportunities availed, transfer effected, training courses attended, disciplinary actions, if any, recorded and personnel appraisal ratings. (2) Personnel Appraisal: The main purpose of any personnel appraisal plan is to help the employee to know his strengths and weaknesses, opportunities and threats (SWOT) and in order to build him for meeting ever increasing job challenges. Constructive criticism and helpful dialogue are excellent guidance for the employee to gain perspective and mental maturity to perform his allotted tasks skillfully and rise in the organization ladder. Companies rate many items pertaining to an individual and we give below an excerpt which will give a good idea of this concept.

Item Rated	Number of Times Found in 50 Merit-Rating Forms*
Group 1: The Old Standbys	
Quantity of work	44
Quality of work	31
Group 2: Job Knowledge and Performance	
Knowledge of job	25
Attendance	14
Punctuality	12
Safety habits	7
Good housekeeping	3
Group 3: Characteristics of the Individual	
Cooperativeness	36
Dependability	35
Initiative	27
Intelligence	17
Accuracy	14
Industry	14
Adaptability	14
Attitude	13
Personality	13
Judgment	12
Application	10
Leadership	6
Conduct	6
Resourcefulness	6
Health	5
Neatness	5
Appearance	4
Enthusiasm	4
Potential	4

*Integrity, loyalty, speech, tact and thoroughness were rated by three or fewer companies.
Source: "Marks of the Good Worker," National Industrial Conference Board Management Record, Vol. 18, No. 5 (May 1956), 168-70

Most companies have their own appraisal methods but the data normally sought to rate belongs to any one of the elements given above.

Good companies normally rate the person on the basis of his job-performance, attitude and behavior and the call the individual for personal counseling.

There are many methods of job evaluation and let us discuss some of them:

(1) Ranking system: In this jobs are ranked on the basis of responsibilities and duties and their importance to overall company objectives. Salary/wages are determined accordingly.

(2) Classification method: They define grades for requirements that are found common to various tasks on the basis of comparison between requirements regarding each task; they are classified with relevant grades.

(3) Points system: Requirements appropriate to each job are analyzed and quantified. Job requirements are subdivided into smaller degrees and each degree is assigned points. The total points a job gets determines its relative position vis-à-vis the job structure.

(4) Factor Comparison: For a few predetermined key jobs, points are allotted and wage rates for such key jobs are fixed. This will serve as a guiding factor for grading other jobs. Let us see three jobs of an organization now:

Job Requirements	Maximum Points	Maintenance Person	Machine Operator	Store Clerk
Experience	20.00	10.00	15.00	5.00
Job Knowledge and Job Skill	40.00	35.00	20.00	10.00
Negligence	20.00	15.00	10.00	5.00
Working Conditions	20.00	5.00	5.00	5.00
	100.00	65.00	50.00	25.00

The above organization fixes a basic pay of say $200 for all categories per month. In addition decides to pay $2 per point as per the above evaluation in which case the 3 job-men will receive:

	Maintenance Person $	Machine Operator $	Store Clerk $
Basic	200	200	200
Points Payment	130 (65*2)	100 (50*2)	50 (25*2)
	330.00	300.00	250.00

COLLECTIVE BARGAINING

Unions are formal associations of employees formed with a view to represent employees in any dialogue to bargain collectively with the management. Their negotiations with the management include improved working conditions, better wage structures, lesser hours of work, more rest periods, etc., and generally work towards establishing good labor policies. In the USA 'organized' labor is a term normally used to distinguish members of unions from employees who do not have a formal union to support them. There are blue collar as well as white-collar worker unions in the USA. Dale Yoder, in his magnum opus "Personnel Management and Industrial Relations," has given the following as the most widely accepted general policies of American Unions:

"...

1.   *To bargain collectively and to expand and increase the scope of the collective bargaining system.*

2.   *To maintain and expand the security and survival capacity of unions and their ability to withstand attacks, and to back up demands with solidarity as well as economic resources.*

3.   *To gain and maintain exclusive control of labor supplies in particular labor markets as a means of enforcing union demands for what are regarded as appropriate working conditions.*

4.   *To improve the economic status and welfare of union members, increasing their earnings and relative shares in national income and their influence, both in employment and in the larger societies in which they are members.*

5.   *To develop and improve the union's arsenal of weapons – programs, practices and techniques to be used in conflict and defense of the organization and in expanding its power.*

6.   *To represent members in the area of political action, identifying candidates and officeholders who are friendly or unfriendly, lobbying and securing political concessions for unions and their members.*

7.   *To maintain a strong organization, democratically controlled but with enough internal discipline to implement such policies as have been described above.*

8.   *To facilitate improved member understanding of union policies and programs and increase skill and competence on the part of union officers by appropriate educational programs..."*

TRAINING AND DEVELOPMENT

Training can be considered as a program built primarily to assist employee development. There are various kinds of training in vogue: (1) Apprenticeship (2) Refresher courses (3) Promotional training (4) On the job training (5) Off the job training, etc.

The specific purposes behind training are:

(1) Knowledge and skill enhancement

(2) Makes it possible to introduce new methods. Encourages people to introduce new methods thereby making it possible for the personnel to work more effectively and efficiently.

(3) Knowledge on safety. It provides the much needed knowledge on how to operate machines without any risk whatsoever.

(4) Latest techniques: Training impacts latest techniques available and makes the operator much more skilful and technique-oriented.

(5) Morale boosting: Promotes self-confidence of personnel as they are trained in skills, knowledge, aptitude and attitude necessary to do their job most efficiently.

(6) Self-actualization: It paves the way for employees to realize their full potential.

Many corporate business houses have substantial training budgets to augment and fine tune their managerial skills. On the job training for managers include:

(1) Planned progression
(2) Temporary promotion
(3) Job rotation
(4) The committee method
(5) Coaching

Training needs are to be analyzed before arriving at the training program. How is need analyzed? A hypothetical case study:

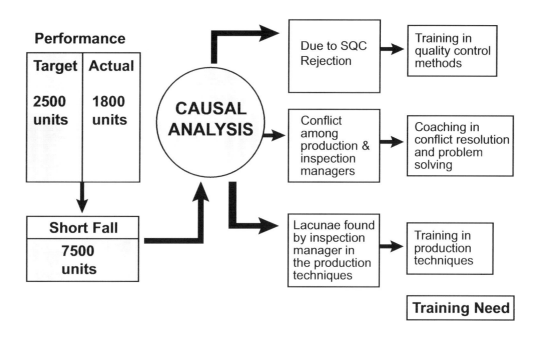

TRAINING NEED ANALYSIS

Training may consist of:

1) Coaching

2) Conference

3) Group dynamics

4) Idea tracking

5) Managerial games

6) Multimedia presentations

7) Role playing

8) Programmed learning

9) T Group

10) Workshop, and

11) Special tuition

ORGANIZATIONAL DEVELOPMENT – OD

Organizational development – simply OD – is a methodical, integrated and a well thought out and well planned approach that seeks to improve organizational effectiveness. The design generally reveals solutions to problems that threaten or are already impeding operating efficiency of the organization at all levels. It may be ineffective communication, or excessive centralization, or extreme decentralization, and/or even willful apathy amounting to non-cooperation. The solutions to problems are found in team building programs, job enrichment programs, programs meant for organizational behavior modification, or simple MBO (Management by Objective), which we have already seen.

The normal organizational development process first aims to recognize the problems correctly, then diagnoses the problems, then seeks data and information feedback, then begins designing and developing a change strategy with proper interventions and then establishes yardsticks for effective evaluation of the change.

LEGAL CONCERNS

The government's priority is to restrain unlawful activities taking over business and to regulate it in a methodical manner. This is one of the reasons why governments all over the world enact appropriate laws to not only safeguard the interests of business but to restrain them from unlawful activities. They contain rules to regulate business not with a view to suppress free enterprise but with a view to encourage so that they prosper in a free market. There are thousands of rules and procedures a manager has to learn and interpret of Federal government alone. Add to this the State laws, rules and procedures and you have a formidable challenge. In an Industrial setting a Manager has to learn about Factories Act and rules, Payment of Wages Act and rules, Minimum Wages Act and rules, Employee Provident Fund Acts and rules, Payment of Bonus Act and rules, Gratuity Act and rules, Industrial Disputes Act and rules, Trade Unions Act and Rules, Purchase Tax Act, Sales Tax Act, Central and State Excise rules, Customs Acts and Rules, Income Tax Act and rules, Value Added Tax (VAT) rules and procedures, etc. Of course, there may be legal advisers to impart correct interpretation of rules and advise on proper follow up of procedures.

The glass ceiling is a theory that there are theoretical barriers which stop women and minorities from advancing in business areas. Imagine a ladder which reaches up into the sky. It looks like you can climb forever, until you hit a ceiling made of glass, which you can't see but also can't be passed through. For example, statistics show that even when women and men have equal qualifications, it is more often the man who receives the job. Over time the term has come to apply to minority groups as well.

The Civil Rights Act of 1964 bans discrimination based on a person's race, religion, nationality or gender. When it was passed, the act essentially worked to eliminate discriminatory Jim Crow laws in the South, such as the "separate but equal" doctrine. The act bans discrimination in employment, voting and use of public areas.

The National Labor Relations Act guarantees the right of workers to form unions. The formation of unions also allows workers to engage in collective bargaining, which allows the workers to bargain as group to get their demands met. This was important because it is generally more effective than single person to management bargaining.

 # *Operational Aspects of Management*

INFORMATION PROCESSING AND MANAGEMENT

The main managerial function is to get things done by making things happen and not piously hoping for desired results to materialize and wishing problems to evaporate. To get things done through others – the essence of managing – in an organizational backdrop requires precise informational flow for a manager. Without precise information from above and from below, a manager finds it difficult to take proper direction and provide proper action plans.

Today, thanks to the Information Technology Revolution, there is an abundant cascade of information, a veritable information system. Instead of hunting for info today we choose from among a bewildering variety of information on any subject.

A manager needs information in order to effectively focus on the functions such as planning, organizing, directing and controlling. The policies of management in the areas of inventories, customer service, scheduling, etc. are developed from information and data generated from production control functions. Likewise information on the competitors' activities, market standing, competitors' overall strategies, their offer of inducements, their planning to introduce new products, etc., are gleaned from the market by salesmen, by wholesalers, by distributors, by retailers and by friendly salesmen of competitors. Such information whether for production or for marketing is essential for managers to process, analyze and use effectively to succeed in accomplishing overall organizational objectives.

INFORMATION AND DATA PROCESSING IN AN ORGANIZATION

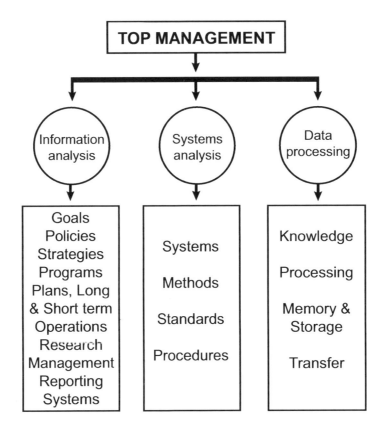

OPERATIONS PLANNING AND CONTROL

A simple illustration of Operations Management

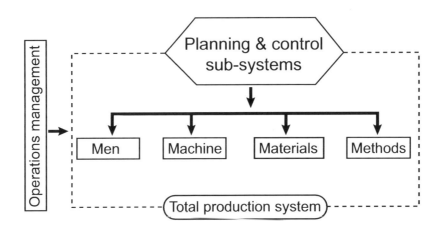

Operations Management can be defined as the planning, organizing, executing and controlling of an organization's total production system through optimal use of the factors that contribute to the planning and control subsystems, viz., Men, Machines, Materials and Methods, and in the process suggesting effective improvement for the total production system.

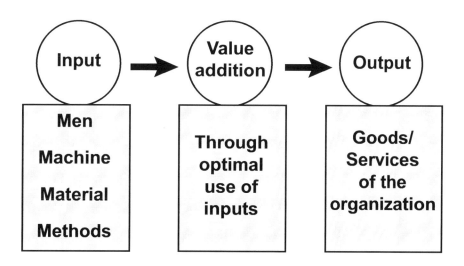

Any production system thinks in terms of excellent customer service, investment on inventory and effective utilization of resources resulting in minimal cost of plant operations. A good production control system always centers around:

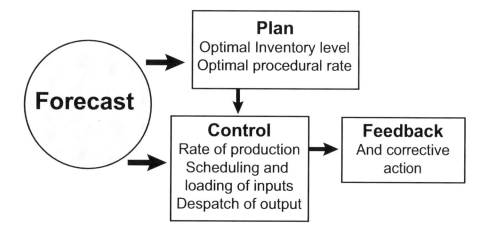

There are a few important steps in Production Planning Forecasting: (1) Preparation of essential information and data (2) Working on the forecast, and (3) Tracking the forecast.

In a factory "Lead time" means the time it takes to get an inventory item – from ordering to arrival and taking into stock. In planning production you have to take into account (a) set up time (b) production time (c) queue time (d) movement time, and (e) waiting time. A typical production plan:

Piston – 4 stroke (in pieces)

Date	Sales	Production	Inventory
Opening Balance	-	-	15,000
10/9/2000	7,000.00	8,000.00	16,000
11/9/2000	5,000.00	10,000.00	21,000
12/9/2000	10,000.00	7,000.00	18,000
13/9/2000	10,000.00	8,000.00	16,000
14/9/2000	9,000.00	9,000.00	16,000
15/9/2000	8,000.00	6,000.00	14,000
Closing Balance	-	-	14,000

PRODUCTIVITY

Productivity is a very complex issue as it depends on a host of variables, some of which may not be easily predictable and therefore must be taken into account. The design of the job itself is a complex factor. Technology is another. Human and managerial facts lend more complexity. Add to these the external factors; you have an issue which is complex and sophisticated at the same time. In its rudimentary equation, productivity relates to the input-output ratio meant for a given time period. The constant factor of course is quality as there is no compromise on that score in any organization. If given expression, a productivity equation looks like the one given below:

Productivity = Output/Input

Suppose, a tailor, Mr. X, in a normal shift of 8 hours stitches 40 medium sized shirts. Mr. X's productivity 40/8 = 5 shirts per machine hour. The productivity here is measured in terms of units produced per machine hour worked. Increased effectiveness and total efficiency are the hallmarks of increased productivity.

TOTAL QUALITY MANAGEMENT (TQM)

Quality of a product determines its salability. Products enjoying exceptional quality standards demand a premium. There should be a conscious effort to maintain a high quality in not only the end product, but even the methods, systems, communication and thinking of top level to the floor level employee. A good quality program includes:

(1) Determination of standards of quality

(2) Institution of an effective continuous on the job checking program with responsibilities and accountability firmly fixed

(3) A recording system for comparing errors vs. standards

(4) A method which spells out corrective action, and

(5) To install a program of analysis and quality improvement whenever found needed.

Checking on the production line while the job is on is a good system. However, it may not be possible to check every piece produced. Here the statistical quality methods come to help. Normally checking is done on a random basis (Random Sampling Method). The most common program liked by organizations is the acceptance sampling method. A sample, normally 10 to 15% of a batch from a running production line, is checked. If they find that a high majority of the checked batch quantities consistently match the set standards for qualitative accuracy, the entire batch (the balance of 90 to 85% as the case may be) is accepted. This is acceptance sampling in essence.

Today there is ISO-9000 (which tells us that a well thought out system will produce predicted quality consistently, with consistency in the implementation of the system at every stage – not only in design or production but in policies and actions of all employees), TQM – Total Quality Management (which tells us to continuously meet agreed customer requirements at the lowest cost, by realizing the potential of employees).

SIX SIGMA

Six Sigma is a finite, controlled, measured plan that a company adheres to in order to be as perfect as possible, with as little defects, returns, etc., as possible. The six comes from their methodology, no more than six standard deviations from the mean (average) of a statistic to their end result. What does that really mean? It means that when a product is rated six sigma, the product exhibits no more than 3.4 non conformities (defects) per million opportunities (NPMO) at the part and process levels. The methodology is broken down into two sub-methodologies the DMAIC and DMADV. The Six Sigma DMAIC process stands for define, measure, analyze, improve, and control. This is used to improve existing policies and procedures.

The Six Sigma DMADV stands for define, measure, analyze, design, and verify. This set is used to develop a brand new product or procedure. All these concepts aim to give a zero-defect product.

The quality movement has acquired many gurus. Chief among them are: (1) Phillip B. Crosby – who always emphasized "zero-defect," (2) Dr W. Edwards Deming – who is considered the forefather of Japanese quality revolution and the thrust of his philosophy has always been planned reduction of variation, and (3) Dr. Joseph Juran who always thought and taught that quality is achievable through people rather than technique. The Six Sigma Concept (which tells us that, when a product is rated as Six Sigma, it means that the product exhibits no more than 3.4 non conformities per million opportunities (NPMO) at the part and process levels). All these concepts aim to give a zero-defect product.

WORK SCHEDULING

An effective and most efficient production control system always assigns a prominent role to work scheduling. There are input scheduling and output scheduling. In input scheduling input control is divided into:

(1) Order Selection i.e., the right orders for feeding into the machines. This is based on planned production rate or customs order, or material control system.

(2) Scheduling – after considering the operations to be performed on each production order, they allot times and arrive at the completion date.

(3) Loading – this involves the working out of hours required to perform each operation and then compares that factor with availability of work hours in each cost (work) center. The capacity planning vis-à-vis the machine, operations, operator, etc., tells you what would be your job flow rate. Let us see the normal scheduling steps:

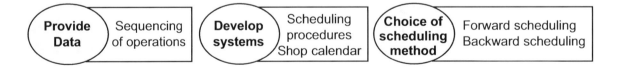

In scheduling one has to: (1) multiply order quality by time per each operation. (2) To the number arrived at 1, add time of transit, and (3) provide for unexpected delays converting it to hours and add to total of 1+2.

Forward Scheduling: Starts today and works out the schedule date for each operation in order to find out the completion date for the order.

Backward Scheduling: Starts with the date on which the completed order is needed in the stores department for shipping, then works out backwards to determine the relevant release date for the order.

OPEN AND CLOSED SYSTEMS

Open systems and closed systems are two different types of work environments. An open system interacts with other systems and exchanges information and materials. For example, a payroll company would be an open system. It must communicate with a number of other companies to stay in business. Also, a factory would have to respond to supply and demand and adjust its output accordingly. A closed system is self contained and doesn't interact with other systems. If a factory were to proceed regardless of supply and demand, it could be considered a closed system.

Sample Test Questions

1) Which of the following is NOT a part of planning?

   A) Setting goals
   B) Setting objectives
   C) Identifying ways to complete objectives
   D) Conducting meetings
   E) Creating departmental goals

The correct answer is D:) Conducting meetings. While conducting meetings is a part of a manager's role, it is not an official role under the planning category which consists of making departmental goals and objectives and determining how those objectives will be accomplished.

2) PERT is an acronym for what?

   A) Personal effort retention training
   B) Practical employment risk training
   C) Program evaluation and review technique
   D) Personnel employment round table
   E) None of the above

The correct answer is C:) Program evaluation and review technique.

3) Which of the following is NOT a part of a PERT chart?

   A) Optimistic time
   B) Pessimistic time
   C) Time expected
   D) Most probable time
   E) None of the above

The correct answer is E:) None of the above. A PERT chart includes a most pessimistic time, a most optimistic time, time expected, and a most probable time.

4) What theory states "organizational change is inevitable and that organizations and people within the organizations have no other choice except following natural law"?

    A) The mechanistic theory
    B) Hierarchy of needs theory
    C) The systems theory
    D) Hawthorne effect theory
    E) None of the above

The correct answer is A:) The mechanistic theory.

5) Which of the following theories argues that the effect of studying something/ someone changes the effects of the study?

    A) The mechanistic theory
    B) Hierarchy of needs theory
    C) The systems theory
    D) Hawthorne effect theory
    E) None of the above

The correct answer is D:) Hawthorne effect theory. This is when the interest in the people's problems affects the outcome, not the changes themselves.

6) Which of the following theories determines interdependence of variables?

    A) The mechanistic theory
    B) Hierarchy of needs theory
    C) The systems theory
    D) Hawthorne effect theory
    E) None of the above

The correct answer is C:) The systems theory. The systems theory deals with interdependence instead of independence of variables and their interactions. It started with a more intensive, very broad, wide-angle – involving a number of variables to measure complex inter-relationships – and inclusive viewpoint. Group behavior is seen in the system as broadly shaped and influenced.

7) Which is the second stage of Maslow's Hierarchy of Needs?

    A) Self-actualization
    B) Esteem needs
    C) Belonging and love
    D) Safety
    E) Physical needs

The correct answer is D:) Safety. Safety is the second stage in Maslow's Hierarchy of Needs.

8) When something is measurable in number it is

    A) Naturalistic observation
    B) Qualitative
    C) Cross sectional studies
    D) Quantitative
    E) Extinction

The correct answer is D:) Quantitative. When something can be measured with numbers, like a completed number of surveys, it is considered quantitative.

9) Who is considered to be the father of modern management?

    A) Abraham Maslow
    B) Max Weber
    C) Chester Barnard
    D) Frederick Herzberg
    E) Peter Drucker

The correct answer is E:) Peter Drucker. Peter Drucker is considered the father of Modern Management.

10) Who completed a study on the fastest and most efficient way to do a job?

    A) Frank Gilbreth
    B) Peter Drucker
    C) Max Weber
    D) Henry Gantt
    E) None of the above

The correct answer is A:) Frank Gilbreth. Frank and Lillian Gilbreth did a study on the most efficient way to do a job.

11) _____ is a way to show the time needed to complete a long or complicated project.

   A) PERT
   B) Critical path method
   C) Bar chart
   D) Gantt chart
   E) Pie chart

The correct answer is D:) Gantt chart. A gantt chart is used to show who will be working on or different stages of a project and the time each step takes.

12) Which person created the five management functions?

   A) Frank Gilbreth
   B) Peter Drucker
   C) Henri Fayol
   D) Max Weber
   E) Henry Gantt

The correct answer is C:) Henri Fayol. Henri Fayol is credited with creating the five management functions which are (1) planning, (2) organizing, (3) commanding, (4) coordinating, and (5) controlling.

13) LPC stands for

   A) Least personnel count
   B) Leverage people credentials
   C) Late potential credit
   D) Least preferred coworker
   E) None of the above

The correct answer is D:) Least preferred coworker. The LPC or least preferred co-worker is an important part of Fiedler's contingency theory.

14) Which of the following are the levels of management?

   A) Technical, interpersonal and conceptual
   B) Technical, interpersonal and line staff
   C) Training, managing, staffing
   D) Controlling, planning, retaining
   E) None of the above

The correct answer is A:) Technical, interpersonal and conceptual.

15) Your company participates in an Affirmative Action program. As a manager you interview two equally individuals for a new position. One candidate is white and one candidate is a pacific islander. What do you do?

   A) Hire the white candidate
   B) Hire the pacific islander candidate
   C) Hire neither and conduct more interviews
   D) Hire towards the quota determined by your HR department
   E) Consult with in house counsel and let them make the decision

The correct answer is D:) Hire towards the quota determined by your HR department. Affirmative Action programs are custom created for each organization in a certain geographic area. Affirmative Action gives minorities, including women, additional opportunities in the workforce.

16) Which of the following is considered a pioneer in management theory?

   A) Peter Drucker
   B) Mary Parker Follet
   C) Frank Gilbreth
   D) Henri Fayol
   E) Frederick Herzberg

The correct answer is B:) Mary Parker Follet. This woman from the late 1800s wrote many books on management theory, and human relations. She also worked as a speaker and volunteer social worker.

17) Which of the following terms illustrates the order of authority in an organization?

   A) Flow chart
   B) PERT chart
   C) Chain of command
   D) Town hall
   E) None of the above

The correct answer is C:) Chain of command. The chain of command is a term that refers to who reports to who in an organization. An organizational chart would show this as well.

18) In Herzberg's motivation-hygiene theory, the hygiene refers to what?

    A) Cleanliness
    B) Work environment
    C) Satisfiers
    D) Motivators
    E) Dissatisfiers

The correct answer is E:) Dissatisfiers. Herzberg's motivation-hygiene theory basically found what makes an employee satisfied. He called something that was a motivation a satisfier and anything that was a dissatisfier was referred to as hygiene.

19) When you find the answer to your problem but settle for something else is an example of the

    A) Implicit favorite model
    B) Bounded rationality model
    C) Econological model
    D) Morality model
    E) Ethical model

The correct answer is B:) Bounded rationality model.

20) When you choose the solution that has the greatest benefit for you

    A) Implicit favorite model
    B) Bounded rationality model
    C) Econological model
    D) Morality model
    E) Ethical model

The correct answer is C:) Econological model.

21) Which of the following people was associated with the Hawthorne Effect study?

    A) Peter Drucker
    B) Mary Parker Follet
    C) Elton Mayo
    D) Frank Gilbreth
    E) James Smith

The correct answer is C:) Elton Mayo. Elton Mayo is also considered the founder of the Human Relations Movement.

22) If you are an authoritarian, you ascribe to

   A) Theory X
   B) Theory Y
   C) Theory XY
   D) Management theory
   E) None of the above

The correct answer is A:) Theory X.

23) Which of the following is considered the father of strategic planning?

   A) Peter Drucker
   B) Chester Barnard
   C) Elton Mayo
   D) Frank Gilbreth
   E) James Smith

The correct answer is B:) Chester Barnard. Chester Barnard is considered the father of strategic planning.

24) Which of the following developed the Acceptance theory?

   A) Peter Drucker
   B) Chester Barnard
   C) Elton Mayo
   D) Frank Gilbreth
   E) James Smith

The correct answer is B:) Chester Barnard. Chester Barnard felt that the authority did not reside on the person giving the orders, but in the minds and will of the subordinates that determined whether to accept or reject those order from above. If these four areas were met then the employee accepted the task or authority: 1) the employee must understand what is asked of them. 2) they agree that the task is in congruence with the goals of the organization. 3) they agreed that the task was in their own personal interest. 4) they were physically and mentally able to comply.

25) A manager who believes that all people are valuable and want to contribute to their best ability you ascribe to

   A) Theory X
   B) Theory Y
   C) Theory XY
   D) Management theory
   E) None of the above

The correct answer is B:) Theory Y.

26) Which of the following is NOT a contributor to an employee's attitude?

   A) Previous jobs
   B) Education
   C) Peers
   D) Family
   E) None of the above

The correct answer is B:) Education. Education is generally not considered a contributor to an employee's attitude.

27) When someone is producing at standard it is called

   A) Role
   B) Role conflict
   C) Norm
   D) Status
   E) None of the above

The correct answer is C:) Norm. A norm or status quo is considered standard.

28) Who created the contingency theory?

   A) Peter Drucker
   B) Chester Barnard
   C) Elton Mayo
   D) Frank Gilbreth
   E) Fred Fiedler

The correct answer is E:) Fred Fiedler.

29) What standard is the following "Giving monetary values to realized sales"?

   A) Physical standard
   B) Capital standard
   C) Revenue standard
   D) Cost standard
   E) Intangible standard

The correct answer is C:) Revenue standard.

30) What standard is the following "monetary value for the cost of operations, such as machine-hour-costs, cost of material per unit, cost of labor per unit, cost per unit of sales, etc."?

   A) Physical standard
   B) Capital standard
   C) Revenue standard
   D) Cost standard
   E) Intangible standard

The correct answer is D:) Cost standard.

31) What standard is the following "quantified standards at the operating level. Products produced in numbers, in value, material used in weightage and value, labor employed in house and in value, services rendered in value, etc."?

   A) Physical standard
   B) Capital standard
   C) Revenue standard
   D) Cost standard
   E) Intangible standard

The correct answer is A:) Physical standard.

32) Which of the following is NOT one of Henry Mintzberg's classifications of organizations?

A) Simple
B) Complex
C) Organic
D) Stable
E) Dynamic

The correct answer is C:) Organic. Henry Mintzberg classified organizations as either simple, complex, stable or dynamic.

33) A good TQM program does NOT include

A) Determination of standards of quality
B) Institution of an effective continuous on the job checking program with responsibilities and accountability firmly fixed
C) A recording system for comparing errors vs. standards
D) A method which alternatives to solutions
E) To install a program of analysis and quality improvement whenever found needed

The correct answer is D:) A method which alternatives to solutions. A good TQM is made up of: (1) determination of standards of quality, (2) institution of an effective continuous on the job checking program with responsibilities and accountability firmly fixed, (3) a recording system for comparing errors vs. standards, (4) a method which spells out corrective action, and (5) to install a program of analysis and quality improvement whenever found needed.

34) Which of the following is NOT a protected Title VII class?

A) Race
B) Age
C) Sexual preference
D) Religion
E) None of the above

The correct answer is C:) Sexual preference.

35) Which of the following is NOT an example of traditional authority?

A) Supervisor
B) Vice President
C) Bishop
D) Secretary
E) Father

The correct answer is D:) Secretary.

36) Which of the following is responsible for ensuring employee safety?

A) OSHA
B) EEO
C) Department of Labor
D) COBRA
E) FBLA

The correct answer is A:) OSHA.

37) Which of the following is NOT a way to deal with risk?

A) Assuming
B) Avoiding
C) Shifting
D) Deflecting
E) Calculating

The correct answer is D:) Deflecting.

38) Which of the following is an example of environmental stress?

A) Construction noise
B) Strong perfume
C) Peers
D) Broken heating unit
E) None of the above

The correct answer is A:) Construction noise.

39) Which of the following is an example of Maslow's first level of needs?

   A) Food
   B) Car
   C) School
   D) Church
   E) None of the above

The correct answer is A:) Food.

40) Which is the second stage of Maslow's hierarchy of needs?

   A) Self-actualization
   B) Esteem needs
   C) Safety needs
   D) Physical needs
   E) Belonging needs

The correct answer is C:) Safety needs.

41) When you choose the best action for each situation

   A) Situational leadership
   B) Participative leadership
   C) Autocratic leadership
   D) Laissez faire leadership
   E) None of the above

The correct answer is A:) Situational leadership.

42) When a supervisor asks for opinions in making decisions

   A) Situational leadership
   B) Participative leadership
   C) Autocratic leadership
   D) Laissez faire leadership
   E) None of the above

The correct answer is B:) Participative leadership.

43) Which of the following is a union function?

    A) Negotiate pay
    B) Creating new business policies
    C) Budgeting
    D) Creating statistical reports
    E) None of the above

The correct answer is A:) Negotiate pay.

44) Which of the following is an example of Maslow's third level of needs?

    A) Sex
    B) Money
    C) Love
    D) Home
    E) Shoes

The correct answer is C:) Love.

45) Which of the following is NOT part of a training program?

    A) Job sharing
    B) Job rotating
    C) Temporary promotion
    D) Promotion
    E) None of the above

The correct answer is D:) Promotion.

46) Which of the following is an industry commonly known to have line employees?

    A) Automotive
    B) Woodworking
    C) Education
    D) Retail
    E) Hospitality

The correct answer is A:) Automotive.

47) Hands off leadership is also called

   A) Situational leadership
   B) Participative leadership
   C) Autocratic leadership
   D) Laissez faire leadership
   E) None of the above

The correct answer is D:) Laissez faire leadership.

48) Which of the following tells employees and others what is the main purpose of the company is

   A) Vision
   B) Mission statement
   C) Company statement
   D) Business plan
   E) None of the above

The correct answer is B:) Mission statement.

49) A policy can be defined as a _____ action course that serves as a guide for the identified and accepted objectives and goals.

   A) Predefined
   B) Flexible
   C) Necessary
   D) Unknown
   E) None of the above

The correct answer is A:) Predefined.

50) A totalitarian leader

   A) Situational leadership
   B) Participative leadership
   C) Autocratic leadership
   D) Laissez faire leadership
   E) None of the above

The correct answer is C:) Autocratic leadership.

51) The way that people communicate with each other using their bodies

    A) Consideration
    B) Body language
    C) Communication
    D) Charisma
    E) None of the above

The correct answer is B:) Body language.

52) Leadership characteristics that inspire employees is called

    A) Chain of command
    B) Vision
    C) Charisma
    D) Motivation
    E) None of the above

The correct answer is C:) Charisma.

53) Agreement of members of a group on a decision is called

    A) Consensus
    B) Group think
    C) Meetings
    D) Consideration
    E) None of the above

The correct answer is A:) Consensus.

54) Leaders that use group ideas to make decisions

    A) Autocratic
    B) Laissez-faire
    C) Democratic
    D) Trait
    E) None of the above

The correct answer is C:) Democratic.

55) Which is NOT a factor that influences the favorableness of a leader?

    A) Leader-member relations
    B) Task structure
    C) Leader position power
    D) Charisma level
    E) None of the above

The correct answer is D:) Charisma level.

56) A billboard is an example of

    A) Active listening
    B) Two-way communication
    C) One-way communication
    D) Passive communication
    E) None of the above

The correct answer is C:) One-way communication.

57) Leaders that give the group total freedom

    A) Autocratic
    B) Laissez faire
    C) Democratic
    D) Trait
    E) None of the above

The correct answer is B:) Laissez faire.

58) Which of the following is NOT a communication pattern?

    A) Chain
    B) Circle
    C) Wheel
    D) Arc
    E) None of the above

The correct answer is D:) Arc.

59) When someone receives too much information and cannot tell what is important from what is not it is called

    A) Overload
    B) Spam
    C) Decoding information
    D) Rejected information
    E) None of the above

The correct answer is A:) Overload.

60) When someone deliberately tampers with a message, leaving out information, it is called

    A) Overload
    B) Omitting
    C) Y pattern
    D) Highlighting
    E) None of the above

The correct answer is B:) Omitting.

61) Which of the following is NOT a supervisory function?

    A) Marketing
    B) Planning
    C) Staffing
    D) Organizing
    E) None of the above

The correct answer is A:) Marketing.

62) Which of the following is an example of an extrinsic reward?

    A) Raise
    B) Self-esteem
    C) Praise
    D) Personal development
    E) None of the above

The correct answer is A:) Raise.

63) If a plant manager is tasked to reduce costs by 10% this is an example of what kind of goal?

    A) Strategic
    B) Long-term
    C) Tactical
    D) Operational
    E) Realistic

The correct answer is D:) Operational.

64) Which of the following shows the relationship between employees and their peers?

    A) Organizational chart
    B) Gantt chart
    C) Decision tree
    D) Simulation
    E) PERT chart

The correct answer is A:) Organizational chart.

65) Which of the following shows alternate paths for decision making?

    A) Organizational chart
    B) Gantt chart
    C) Decision tree
    D) Simulation
    E) None of the above

The correct answer is C:) Decision tree.

66) When a supervisor administers a questionnaire among participants that have never met it is called

    A) Brainstorming
    B) Sampling
    C) Delphi technique
    D) Groupthink
    E) Questionnaire

The correct answer is C:) Delphi technique.

67) Which of the following shows timelines for projects?

    A) Organizational chart
    B) Gantt chart
    C) Decision tree
    D) Simulation
    E) None of the above

The correct answer is B:) Gantt chart.

68) Who created Theory X and Theory Y?

    A) Max Weber
    B) Abraham Maslow
    C) Douglas McGregor
    D) Frank Gilbreth
    E) Henri Fayol

The correct answer is C:) Douglas McGregor.

69) When two groups or individuals work together to resolve a problem it is called

    A) Negotiation
    B) Grievance
    C) Arbitration
    D) Mediation
    E) None of the above

The correct answer is A:) Negotiation.

70) What is it called when a third party is facilitating negotiations?

    A) Concession
    B) Grievance
    C) Arbitration
    D) Mediation
    E) None of the above

The correct answer is D:) Mediation.

71) An employee that works on an assembly line performing the same task again and again is an example of

    A) Job specialization
    B) Job rotation
    C) Job sharing
    D) Job description
    E) Job requirement

The correct answer is A:) Job specialization.

72) Two receptionists work at Widget, Inc., one in the morning and one in the afternoon. They are an example of

    A) Job specialization
    B) Job rotation
    C) Job sharing
    D) Job control
    E) None of the above

The correct answer is C:) Job sharing.

73) When a person acts as expected as part of the group they are portraying their

    A) Role
    B) Groupthink
    C) Norm
    D) Status rank
    E) Mole

The correct answer is A:) Role.

74) Who first studied job motions with bricklayers, studying how fewer hand motions made the work faster?

    A) Max Weber
    B) Abraham Maslow
    C) Douglas McGregor
    D) Frank Gilbreth
    E) Fredrick Hertzberg

The correct answer is D:) Frank Gilbreth.

75) What is it called when a third party of empowered to resolve a disagreement it is called?

    A) Negotiation
    B) Grievance
    C) Arbitration
    D) Mediation
    E) None of the above

The correct answer is C:) Arbitration.

76) Who was a proponent of bureaucracy?

    A) Max Weber
    B) Abraham Maslow
    C) Douglas McGregor
    D) Frank Gilbreth
    E) Fredrick Hertzberg

The correct answer is A:) Max Weber.

77) Which of the following can NOT be discussed in a job interview?

    A) Education and degrees
    B) Children
    C) Previous wages
    D) Personality
    E) Salary

The correct answer is B:) Children.

78) Which of the following was NOT one of Edward Deming's suggestions?

    A) Decrease the number of employees
    B) Institute training on the job
    C) Have a clear and consistent purpose
    D) Eliminate the need for quality checks
    E) Remove barriers to progress

The correct answer is A:) Decrease the number of employees. Deming believed that most production problems stemmed from inefficient management practices, not employee problems.

79) The grapevine of the organization is everything BUT

    A) Formal
    B) Generally accurate
    C) Verbal
    D) Exists in every organization
    E) None of the above

The correct answer is A:) Formal.

80) What does ERG stand for?

    A) Existentialism Reality Growth
    B) Existence Relatedness Growth
    C) Existence Respect Greatness
    D) Endurance Relatedness Growth
    E) Endurance Reality Greatness

The correct answer is B:) Existence Relatedness Growth. The ERG theory is so named for its three levels.

81) When a supervisor believes that all employees like work it is called

    A) Theory Y
    B) Theory X
    C) Hawthorne effect
    D) TQM
    E) Humanistic theory

The correct answer is A:) Theory Y.

82) Which of the following describes the break even point?

    A) Profits + expenses < 0
    B) Profits x expenses > 0
    C) Expenses / profits < 0
    D) Expenses - profits = 0
    E) Expenses - profits > 0

The correct answer is D:) Expenses - profits = 0. At this point the business neither makes nor loses money.

83) This scientific study originally tested worker's output and light, later revealing unintended consequences

   A) Theory Y
   B) Theory X
   C) Hawthorne effect
   D) TQM
   E) Contingency theory

The correct answer is C:) Hawthorne effect.

84) Which of the following types of discrimination does the Civil Rights Act of 1964 NOT ban?

   A) Laissez faire leadership
   B) Race
   C) Nationality
   D) Gender
   E) All of the above are addressed by the Civil Rights Act of 1964

The correct answer is E:) All of the above are addressed by the Civil Rights Act of 1964. The Civil Rights Act of 1964 bans discrimination based on a person's race, religion, nationality or gender.

85) Referent power is the same as

   A) Lassaize faire leadership
   B) Charismatic leadership
   C) Peer pressure
   D) Expert leadership
   E) None of the above

The correct answer is B:) Charismatic leadership.

86) Which of the following describes chain of command?

    A) An increase in the price of an object before it is sold.
    B) A plan for how money will be used effectively.
    C) A listing of what a job includes such as tasks, duties and responsibilities.
    D) The hierarchy through which decisions are made, responsibility lies, and power flows.
    E) Programs which are used to help managers work and organize more efficiently.

The correct answer is D:) The hierarchy through which decisions are made, responsibility lies, and power flows. The chain of command emphasizes the vertical structure of an organization, or in other words the relationships between leader and subordinate.

87) Legitimate power is the same as

    A) Laissez faire leadership
    B) Traditional leadership
    C) Peer pressure
    D) Expert leadership
    E) None of the above

The correct answer is B:) Traditional leadership.

88) What is meant by the statement "you can delegate authority but not responsibility?"

    A) Managers have the right to delegate assignments and projects to other people, but the responsibility will always lie with them.
    B) Managers can delegate assignments and projects to other people, but they cannot force those people to be responsible and get them done.
    C) Managers cannot delegate assignments to other people. They can just tell everyone that the person was responsible for getting it done.
    D) Managers can neither delegate the right nor responsibility to get something done.
    E) None of the above

The correct answer is A:) Managers have the right to delegate assignments and projects to other people, but the responsibility will always lie with them.

89) Regarding sexual harassment which of the following is NOT true

    A) Offenders can be same or opposite sex
    B) Victims do not have to be harassed personally but affected through environment
    C) Harasser must be a superior employee
    D) Harassment may occur without economic injury
    E) None of the above

The correct answer is C:) Harasser must be a superior employee.

90) Which of the following is NOT one of the categories of managerial roles?

    A) Decision roles
    B) Informational roles
    C) Interpersonal roles
    D) Conceptual roles
    E) None of the above

The correct answer is D:) Conceptual roles. Conceptual skills are needed, but decisional, information and interpersonal are the three roles.

91) Who created a system of human needs and motivations?

    A) Max Weber
    B) Abraham Maslow
    C) Douglas McGregor
    D) Frank Gilbreth
    E) Peter Drucker

The correct answer is B:) Abraham Maslow.

92) Which of the following describes management information systems?

    A) An increase in the price of an object before it is sold.
    B) A plan for how money will be used effectively.
    C) A listing of what a job includes such as tasks, duties and responsibilities.
    D) The hierarchy through which decisions are made, responsibility lies, and power flows.
    E) Programs which are used to help managers work and organize more efficiently.

The correct answer is E:) Programs which are used to help managers work and organize more efficiently.

93) Long term success through customer satisfaction

    A) Theory Y
    B) Theory X
    C) Hawthorne effect
    D) TQM
    E) Contingency theory

The correct answer is D:) TQM.

94) Which of the following is NOT a step in the decision making process according to Herbert Simon?

    A) Intelligence
    B) Satisfice
    C) Identify
    D) Design
    E) All of the above are correct

The correct answer is C:) Identify. Identification of the problem occurs in the intelligence stage.

95) Who was responsible for developing the 14 principles of management?

    A) Max Weber
    B) Henri Fayol
    C) Douglas McGregor
    D) Frank Gilbreth
    E) Peter Drucker

The correct answer is B:) Henri Fayol.

96) Which of the following does the Upstream Capital Costs Index NOT track?

    A) Equipment
    B) Facilities
    C) Opportunities
    D) Materials
    E) Personnel

The correct answer is C:) Opportunities. This is, however, a factor in SWOT analysis.

97) Which of the following are barriers to making decisions?

    A) Statistics
    B) Lack of statistics
    C) Emotions
    D) All of the above
    E) None of the above

The correct answer is D:) All of the above.

98) An employee knows that if they do well on a presentation they will receive a promotion which they want more than anything else. They believe that there is an 85% chance that they will do well on the presentation. According to Vroom's Expectancy Theory, what is their motivation level?

    A) -.85
    B) -.25
    C) 0
    D) .25
    E) .85

The correct answer is E:) .85. Their expectancy level would be .85, valency would be 1 and instrumentality would be 1. (.85)(1)(1)=.85.

99) Which of the following is NOT a type of resistance?

    A) Logical
    B) Psychological
    C) Sociological
    D) Biological
    E) All of the above

The correct answer is D:) Biological.

100) Which of the following correctly interprets the two factor model in context?

    A) A person who is very dissatisfied with the cleanliness of their work environment will become much happier with their job if it becomes cleaner.
    B) A person becomes happy with their job when they feel responsibility and accomplishment, but they will not be unhappy without them.
    C) A person who does not receive benefits from there job will feel a lot better about their job once they begin to receive them.
    D) A person who is recognized for their job on a regular basis will become dissatisfied and upset if the praise discontinues.
    E) None of the above

The correct answer is B:) A person becomes happy with their job when they feel responsibility and accomplishment, but they will not be unhappy without them. According to Herzberg, satisfaction and dissatisfaction are classified by two separate types of factors. A single factor cannot change a person from being happy to being unhappy with their job.

101) Which is the first stage of Lewin's stages of change?

    A) Freeze
    B) Unfreeze
    C) Transition
    D) Slushiness
    E) None of the above

The correct answer is A:) Freeze.

102) Who does performance appraisals?

    A) Fellow employees
    B) Unbiased volunteers
    C) Managers or supervisors
    D) Individuals
    E) None of the above

The correct answer is C:) Managers or supervisors. Performance appraisals are used to determine an employee's efficiency and abilities. It may result in a raise if the employee is doing well, or being fired or sent to additional training if they do poorly.

103) Who believed that managers make decisions based on their assumptions of human nature?

    A) McGregor
    B) Taylor
    C) Ratter
    D) Johnson
    E) Maslow

The correct answer is A:) McGregor.

104) Which of the following is job description?

    A) A listing of what a job includes such as tasks, duties and responsibilities.
    B) An evaluation of the importance and effectiveness of a job in relation to a company as a whole.
    C) How essential job tasks are related to the job.
    D) Breaking tasks into simplified and specialized components.
    E) None of the above

The correct answer is A:) A listing of what a job includes such as tasks, duties and responsibilities. Job evaluation is described in B and job specialization is described in D.

105) When an interest in the people's problems affects the outcome, not the changes themselves, it is known as

    A) Hawthorne effect
    B) Taylor effect
    C) Laissez faire effect
    D) Groupthink effect
    E) Hygiene theory

The correct answer is A:) Hawthorne effect.

106) Which of the following is NOT a level of management according to Henri Fayol?

    A) Planning
    B) Organization
    C) Commanding
    D) Coordinating
    E) All of the above are levels of management

The correct answer is E:) All of the above are levels of management. Henri Fayol's identified six levels of management functions. These levels are forecasting, planning, organization, commanding, coordinating and controlling.

107) Factor that always stays the same

    A) Dependent variable
    B) Independent variable
    C) Constant
    D) Correlation
    E) Statistic

The correct answer is C:) Constant.

108) Which of the following is NOT one of the three qualities a good manager should possess?

    A) Conceptual skills
    B) Diagnostic skills
    C) Technical skills
    D) Interpersonal skills
    E) None of the above

The correct answer is B:) Diagnostic skills. The three qualities are conceptual skills, technical skills and interpersonal skills.

109) Information that is difficult to measure is called

    A) Quantitative
    B) Qualitative
    C) Longitudinal
    D) Dependent
    E) Constant

The correct answer is B:) Qualitative.

110) A flat organization is an organization with

    A) A high ratio of mid level management to high level management positions.
    B) A low ratio of mid level management to low level employee positions.
    C) A low number (if any) of mid level management positions.
    D) A high ratio of low level employees to potential customers.
    E) None of the above

The correct answer is C:) A low number (if any) of mid level management positions. This way the top level management comes into direct contact with the low level employees.

111) Which of the following is NOT a part of Kurt Lewin's change model?

    A) Unfreeze
    B) Transition
    C) Freeze
    D) Slushiness
    E) None of the above

The correct answer is E:) None of the above. Lewin's change model includes all of the above answer choices.

112) Which of the following describes the difference between line and staff positions?

    A) Line positions are directly involved in creating profit, whereas staff positions do the maintenance or supporting jobs.
    B) Staff positions are directly involved to creating profit, whereas line positions do the maintenance or supporting jobs.
    C) Line positions are responsible for manufacturing and staff positions are responsible for sales.
    D) Staff positions are responsible for manufacturing and line positions are responsible for sales.
    E) None of the above

The correct answer is A:) Line positions are directly involved in creating profit, whereas staff positions do the maintenance or supporting jobs. Line positions would be involved in manufacturing and sales, whereas staff positions involve payrolls or other supporting types of jobs.

113) Standards or principles

   A) Norms
   B) Values
   C) Rules
   D) Status quo
   E) Groups

The correct answer is B:) Values.

114) Which of the following describes budget?

   A) An increase in the price of an object before it is sold.
   B) A plan for how money will be used effectively.
   C) A listing of what a job includes such as tasks, duties and responsibilities.
   D) The hierarchy through which decisions are made, responsibilities lies, and power flows.
   E) Programs which are used to help managers work and organize more efficiently.

The correct answer is B:) A plan for how money will be used effectively. A budget helps to organize and track the flow of money in a company.

115) Which of the following is NOT a factor with job satisfaction?

   A) Hours
   B) Pay
   C) Benefits
   D) Vacation location
   E) Working conditions

The correct answer is D:) Vacation location.

116) Which of the following is an open system?

I. A clothing store which operates in a busy mall.
II. A factory which continuously produces product.
III. An advertisement company.

A) I only
B) I and III only
C) II and III only
D) I and III only
E) I, II and III

The correct answer is B:) I and III only. Both the clothing store and the advertisement company must directly interact and respond to occurrences in the market.

117) When a person responds to a neutral stimulus _____ is being used.

A) Classical conditioning
B) Operant conditioning
C) Extrinsic reinforcer
D) Intrinsic reinforcer
E) None of the above

The correct answer is A:) Classical conditioning.

118) Which of the following is NOT a way of showing social responsibility?

A) Recycling
B) Goodwill
C) Public relations
D) Revenue generation
E) None of the above

The correct answer is D:) Revenue generation. Social responsibility is the idea that a business is part of something bigger than itself. It is part of a global community. With that knowledge comes the responsibility to do what is best for the company and for society as well. Some of the ways that companies can contribute to society are making environmentally friendly choices as well as contributing to charities.

119) Clayton Alderfer created his ERG theory based on the work of which theorist?

    A) Max Weber
    B) Henri Fayol
    C) Abraham Maslow
    D) Frank Gilbreth
    E) Peter Drucker

The correct answer is C:) Abraham Maslow. Alderfer wanted to revise Maslow's Hierarchy of Needs to match empirical research.

120) Which of the following acts guarantees the right of workers to form unions?

    A) National Union Legalization Act
    B) Civil Rights Act 1964
    C) National Labor Relations Act
    D) Collective Organizations Act
    E) None of the above

The correct answer is C:) National Labor Relations Act. The formation of unions also allows workers to engage in collective bargaining.

121) When you are a secretary and there are seven levels between your role and the CEO, your organization is considered to be

    A) Fat
    B) Tall
    C) Flat
    D) Short
    E) Huge

The correct answer is B:) Tall.

122) Which of the following best describes the glass ceiling?

    A) A literal physical barrier which stops people from accessing the top floor of a building without proper identification.
    B) A legislative barrier which stops too many immigrants from entering the country.
    C) A legislative barrier which stops people from accessing information about government operations.
    D) A theoretical barrier which stops women and minorities from advancing in business areas.
    E) None of the above

The correct answer is D:) A theoretical barrier which stops women and minorities from advancing in business areas. For example, statistics show that even when women and men have equal qualifications, it is more often the man who receives the job.

123) The CEO of a major corporation giving a talk show interview is an example of

    A) Advertising
    B) Goodwill
    C) Public relations
    D) Revenue generation
    E) None of the above

The correct answer is C:) Public relations.

124) Which theory advocates increasing production by breaking down production into simplified processes?

    A) Expectancy Model
    B) ERG Theory
    C) Taylorism
    D) Two Factor Model
    E) None of the above

The correct answer is C:) Taylorism. Taylor encouraged breaking jobs from complex processes into step-by-step patterns of production.

125) If you believe that all people are good – you ascribe to this school of thought

    A) Biological
    B) Cognitive
    C) Structuralism
    D) Humanistic
    E) Cultural

The correct answer is D:) Humanistic.

126) The organizational structure where organizations are divided by products or divisions

    A) Functional
    B) Line and staff
    C) Product
    D) Matrix
    E) None of the above

The correct answer is C:) Product.

127) Six Sigma strives for

    A) Perfect attendance
    B) Improvements in ethnic quotas
    C) Less environmental impact
    D) Perfection in processes and product
    E) None of the above

The correct answer is D:) Perfection in processes and product. For a company to be a perfect Six Sigma, they must have no more than 3.4 defects per million opportunities.

128) Herzberg believed that increasing which of the following would increase job satisfaction?

    A) Breadth
    B) Job enlargement
    C) Hygiene
    D) Depth

The correct answer is D:) Depth. Depth is related to job enrichment, which was Herzberg's focus.

129) When a person is responsible for the outcome of completing a task well it is called

    A) Sociological
    B) ERG Theory
    C) Indefensible
    D) Accountable
    E) None of the above

The correct answer is D:) Accountable.

130) Which of the following is NOT a part of the path-goal theory?

    A) Provides a clear path
    B) Helps remove barriers to the problems
    C) Increases the rewards along the route
    D) Increases the rewards at the end of the route
    E) None of the above

The correct answer is E:) None of the above. All of the above answer choices are a part of the path-goal theory.

131) Which are friendships which cause the development of in-groups and out-groups?

    A) Unions
    B) Fraternities
    C) Vertical-dyad linkages
    D) Group contributions
    E) None of the above

The correct answer is C:) Vertical-dyad linkages. These are friendships which cause the development of in-groups and out-groups in a working environment. The in-groups receive favorable treatment such as interesting assignments, promotions and raises. The out-groups are the groups which do not share the mutual respect and obligations of a vertical-dyad linkage, and therefore are at a disadvantage. In-group workers tend to be more productive and enthusiastic.

132) Which of the following statements is FALSE?

    A) Type B personalities are generally less efficient than Type A personalities because they are so relaxed.
    B) Type A personalities and type B personalities are both efficient, they just do things different ways.
    C) Type B personalities are laid back and casual, which makes them unhealthy and increases their risks.
    D) Type A personalities are generally less efficient than Type B personalities because they have so many focuses that they never get any one project finished.
    E) None of the above

The correct answer is B:) Type A personalities and type B personalities are both efficient, they just do things different ways.

133) The hot stove method of discipline includes which of the following?

    A) A warning
    B) Immediate discipline/consequence
    C) Consistent application
    D) All of the above
    E) None of the above

The correct answer is D:) All of the above.

Test Taking Strategies

Here are some test-taking strategies that are specific to this test and to other CLEP tests in general:

- Keep your eyes on the time. Pay attention to how much time you have left.
- Read the entire question and read all the answers. Many questions are not as hard to answer as they may seem. Sometimes, a difficult sounding question really only is asking you how to read an accompanying chart. Chart and graph questions are on most CLEP tests and should be an easy free point.
- If you don't know the answer immediately, the new computer-based testing lets you mark questions and come back to them later if you have time.
- Read the wording carefully. Some words can give you hints to the right answer. There are no exceptions to an answer when there are words in the question such as always, all or none. If one of the answer choices includes most or some of the right answers, but not all, then that is not the correct answer. Here is an example:

    The primary colors include all of the following:

        A) Red, Yellow, Blue, Green
        B) Red, Green, Yellow
        C) Red, Orange, Yellow
        D) Red, Yellow, Blue
        E) None of the above

    Although item A includes all the right answers, it also includes an incorrect answer, making it incorrect. If you didn't read it carefully, were in a hurry, or didn't know the material well, you might fall for this.
- Make a guess on a question that you do not know the answer to. There is no penalty for an incorrect answer. Eliminate the answer choices that you know are incorrect. For example, this will let your guess be a 1 in 3 chance instead.

What Your Score Means

Based on your score, you may, or may not, qualify for credit at your specific institution. At University of Phoenix, a score of 50 is passing for full credit. At Utah Valley State College, the score is unpublished, the school will accept credit on a case-by-case basis. Another school, Brigham Young University (BYU) does not accept CLEP credit. To find out what score you need for credit, you need to get that information from your school's website or academic advisor.

You can score between 20 and 80 on any CLEP test. Some exams include percentile ranks. Each correct answer is worth one point. You lose no points for unanswered or incorrect questions.

Test Preparation

How much you need to study depends on your knowledge of a subject area. If you are interested in literature, took it in school, or enjoy reading then your studying and preparation for the literature or humanities test will not need to be as intensive as for someone who is new to literature.

This book is much different than the regular CLEP study guides. This book actually teaches you the information that you need to know to pass the test. If you are particularly interested in an area, or feel like you want more information, do a quick search online. We've tried not to include too much depth in areas that are not as essential on the test. Everything in this book will be on the test. It is important to understand all major theories and concepts listed in the table of contents. It is also very important to know any bolded words.

Don't worry if you do not understand or know a lot about the area. With minimal study, you can complete and pass the test.

Specific Test Details

This test is approximately 100 multiple-choice questions that need to be answered in 90 minutes. This test, depending on your university, is usually worth 3 credit hours.

Legal Note

FLASHCARDS

This section contains flashcards for you to use to further your understanding of the material and test yourself on important concepts, names or dates. Read the term or question then flip the page over to check the answer on the back. Keep in mind that this information may not be covered in the text of the study guide. Take your time to study the flashcards, you will need to know and understand these concepts to pass the test.

Management Theory: Empirical/Case Approach

Management Theory: Interpersonal Behavior Approach

Management Theory: Group Behavior Approach

Management Theory: Cooperative Social Systems Approach

Management Theory: Sociotechnical Systems Approach

Management Theory: Decision Theory Approach

Management Theory: Systems Approach

Management Theory: Mathematical or Management Science Approach

Understanding people and relationships. If people were understood perfectly, reaching organizational goals would not be difficult.

The experience of past situations guide the present. Find out why an action succeeded or failed by analyzing the basic reasons.

Propounded by Christian Barnard, it is the cooperative interaction of thoughts, ideas, wants and desires of two or more people.

Work in groups rather than in isolation. The study of how behavior patterns in groups affect production.

A manager's most important function is decision making and therefore decisions should be the central focus. All other functions of a manager are built around decisions.

Credited to E.L. Trist, this approach seeks to emphasize the systems aspect of group behavior.

Mathematical models forms part of this theory. Each situation is fraught in terms of available mathematical models and then analyzes the situation threadbare arriving at a mathematically correct decision.

Management is a system, which envelops within itself many subsystems, all operating within the total environment.

Management Theory: Contingency or Situational Approach

Management Theory: Managerial Roles Approach

Management Theory: Operational Approach

Economic Environment

Technological Environment

Social Environment

Political and Legal Environment

Ethical Environment

Propounded by Professor Henry Mintzberg. Observing what other mangers do, then using such observations as a platform for analyzing and concluding on the basis of such analysis.

Any manager's performance is directly related to a set of given circumstance or contingency. Some theorist also feel that it takes into account not only situations but also on the behavior.

Availability of capital, rate of interest, labor availability and how well things are organized, general price levels, the degree of productivity, the willingness of entrepreneurs and availability of managerial skills.

Imparting knowledge from every other field of knowledge such as sociology, mathematics, economics, psychology etc.

Value systems unique to particular group of people or society. The value system consists of attitudes, behavior patterns, needs, wants, expectations, level of education, the degree of intelligence, general beliefs, customs and traditions.

How good the available knowledge is used through technology is a factor to reckon with. How to conceive ideas, how to design, how to produce optimally, how to effect efficient distribution and how well marketing is done, are technology oriented.

Holding on to moral principles of what is right and what is wrong, guided by value systems prevalent in society and generally behaving in a responsible way.

Laws, rules, regulations, governmental polices that affect an organization.

Social Responsibilities	Steps in Planning
Mechanistic Theory	Systems Theory
Revenue Standards	Frederick Taylor
PERT stands for what?	Self-actualization

Analysis of opportunities. Setting of objectives. Identify the basis. Compare alternatives. Design relevant plans. Quantify for control.

Organizations as well as mangers should be socially responsive to the society as a whole and should be able to do their bit when a situation calls for it.

Organizational processes should be guided and influenced because all things are interdependent.

Organizational change is inevitable and natural processes should be allowed to take their own course.

Scientific management school

Giving monetary value to realized sales

Highest need in Maslow's hierarchy - Level 5

Program evaluation and review technique

Esteem Needs

Belonging and Love

Safety

Physical Needs

Groupthink

Paradox

Synergy

Laissez-faire leader

Level 3 need

Level 4 need

Level 1 need

Level 2 need

Contradictory Conclusion

Conformity in a group situation

Hands off leadership

Cooperative action

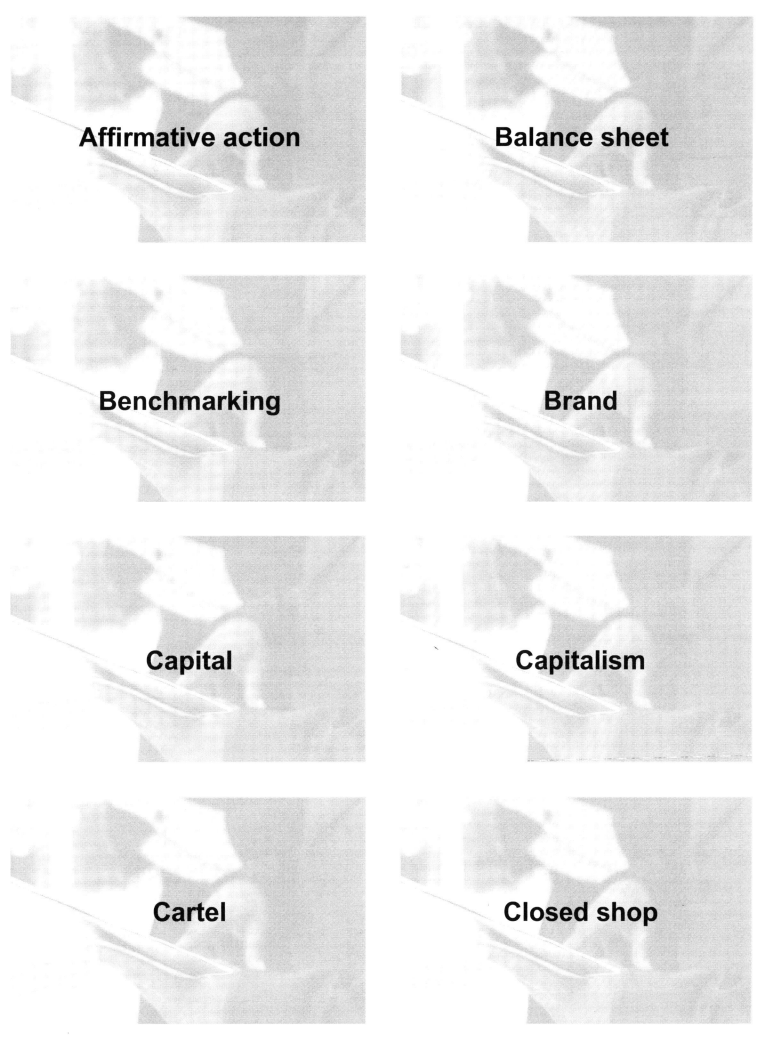

Affirmative action

Balance sheet

Benchmarking

Brand

Capital

Capitalism

Cartel

Closed shop

A summary of a company's finances including debts, what it owns and owner's equity.

A detailed plan that a company makes to recruit and advance women and minorities.

An element which makes one product distinct from others.

Measuring success based on accepted standards.

An economic theory reliant upon competition between businesses.

The money paid by investors or lenders to get a company started.

When an employer must hire only members of a union.

A group of distinct firms that work together essentially creating a monopoly.

Coaching

Collective bargaining

Commission

Compensation

Competition

Controlling

Decentralization

Direct selling

When a group with similar interests bargains as a group.

When the new employee works with the employee they are replacing.

Money given to employees for their work.

When employees are paid rewards based on a percentage of their sales.

Determining if the methods being used adequately match planned results.

Rivalry between companies.

When a product is sold directly to a consumer from a manufacturer.

Delegating authority while still retaining supreme authority.

Directing

Embargo

Entrepreneur

Ergonomics

Featherbedding

Fixed asset

Flextime

Gainsharing plans

Prohibiting trade with foreign nations.

Providing leadership and instructions to employees.

The study of designing more comfortable equipment.

A person who starts a business.

An asset which a company has held for at least one year and cannot easily be transferred to cash.

When unions force employers to pay for unnecessary or uncompleted work.

A sharing of profits among employees and management based on preset formulas.

When workers have a few required hours but can plan their schedules how they wish.

Gantt chart

Glass ceiling

Globalization

Gross domestic product

Gross margin

Group interview

Hawthorne effective

Intangible assets

A theoretical barrier to the advancement of women and minorities.

A bar chart which displays timelines for upcoming projects.

The total sales or earnings of a company, ignoring taxes and cost of production.

When a company is in multiple countries using similar market strategies.

Several applicants meet with one or more company representatives.

Net sales - cost

Assets which cannot be quantified or have no physical representation.

When workers are more productive because they know they are being watched.

Job description

Job enlargement

Job enrichment

Job relatedness

Job rotation

Job sharing

Just-in-time inventory management

Law of demand

Increasing the number of tasks an employee must complete.

A listing of what a job includes such as tasks, duties and responsibilities.

How essential job tasks are related to the job.

Improving employee satisfaction by increasing the number of responsibilities or tasks.

When two or more individuals trade off hours for one full time job.

Moving employees from one department to another to increase their skills.

There is an inverse relationship between supply and demand.

An inventory management system in which inventory arrives only when it is needed.

Line authority

Line staff organization

Management by objectives

Markup

Nepotism

NLRA

Norris-LaGuardia Act

On-the-job training

The presence of both line and staff authority in an organization.

The path authority follows in a chain of command.

An increase in the price of an product before it is sold.

When employees and management define goals and work to achieve them.

National Labor Relations Act

The tendency to hire relatives of current employees.

When you learn the job by actually doing it.

Made "yellow-dog" contracts unenforceable.

Patent	**Personnel management**
Piece rate	**Poison pill**
Retained earnings	**Scalar principle**
Small Business Administration	**Staffing**

Deals with recruitment, selection, placement, training, compensation and working conditions.

A legal document giving exclusive rights to produce a product to one person or company.

Any strategy used by a company to make its stock less attractive.

Total weekly earnings divided by the total number of hours worked that week.

The belief that there should be a clearly defined chain of command.

The profit which is kept and used by the company.

A systematic method of filling a position in an organization structure.

A government agency created to protect small businesses.

Theory X

Theory Y

Time utility

Tort

Underemployment

Unemployment insurance

Unions

Yellow dog contract

States that people enjoy work and work better with little supervision.

States that people dislike work and therefore must be closely supervised.

The illegal infringement of a right.

The added value of a product due to convenience.

Provides weekly pay to employees who lose their job.

When people work jobs that are below their skill level.

A promise from an employee to not join a union as a condition for getting hired.

Formal associations of employees to represent employees in negotiations with management.